CONTENTS

PREFACE

The creation of County Councils in 1888 led to the setting up of County Record Offices, principally to preserve and conserve the records of the Quarter Sessions. These records are the oldest public records of the historic counties of England and Wales that survive - in some counties from the middle of the fifteenth century through to 1972, when the Quarter Sessions were replaced by Crown Courts.

For many years, Quarter Sessions records have been neglected by both family and local historians despite the publication of some excellent guides to their contents by county record offices and record societies. However, the growth of the Internet and work on transcribing and indexing has made many more aware of the importance of these records as a major source for family and local historical research.

To find out what business was transacted at the Quarter Sessions for a particular county the researcher should start by checking the Minute Books. These books are also known as the Sessions Books, Order Books or Court Books. Before 1732 many of these were written in Latin. They contain a summary of the business that had been transacted and show that the Quarter Sessions dealt with administrative cases as well as judicial cases. Many of the administrative duties were introduced during Tudor times, especially those associated with the Poor Law Acts of 1597 and 1601. Categories to be found amongst these are listed on the inside back cover.

The "golden age" of Quarter Sessions records is the period from 1732 until the middle of the nineteenth century. By that time the impact of legislation passed by the Reform Parliament of 1832 and its successors was beginning to have a major impact on Quarter Sessions business, by considerably reducing the administrative duties of the Justices of the Peace. Consequently this Guide does not mention as many records after 1850. By then there are many alternative sources for family historians to check such as census returns, Certificates of Birth, Marriage and Death, Probate Wills, Workhouse and Asylum records etc.

Local Newspapers, some of which date from the middle of the eighteenth century, are a source which should be checked in parallel with Quarter Sessions papers. These often include detailed reports of judicial cases tried at Quarter Sessions and of course may be easier to read than the handwritten case papers. A selected list of local newspapers that existed from 1750 onwards and survive in the British Library Newspapers Library, in county records offices and local studies libraries can be found in *Local Newspapers 1750-1920 in England and Wales* etc (FFHS 2nd ed. 2002). This and other Gibson Guides relating to several individual classes of records, which appear in Quarter Sessions collections, are listed on the inside front cover of this Guide.

Finally, a reminder that the information in this book was correct at the time of printing but additional information is being posted almost daily on the Internet. Do check the "Access to Archives" [A2] website as well as those of county record offices. See if the records in which you are particularly interested are listed and perhaps have been recently indexed or transcribed. Good hunting!

Richard Ratcliffe

QUARTER SESSIONS
RECORDS
for Family Historians
A select list

The Family History Partnership
2007

Fifth edition published 2007 by
The Family History Partnership
PO Box 502
Bury, Lancashire BL8 9EP

Email: sales@thefamilyhistorypartnership.com
Webpage: www.thefamilyhistorypartnership.com

First edition, 1982.
Second edition, 1983, reprinted 1985, 1986.
Third edition, 1992.
Fourth edition, 1995.
All published by the Federation of Family History Societies

Fifth edition, Copyright © J.S.W. Gibson, 2007.

ISBN 978 1 906280 02 4

Typeset in Aerial from disks prepared by Jeremy Gibson.
Printed by the Alden Press, Witney, Oxon..

Cover illustration: The Royal Arms from a settlement certificate of 1715.

Acknowledgments

This Guide first appeared twenty-five years ago, with three further editions. Plans for a fifth edition started in 2002, when Else Churchill undertook a check of recent accessions to the library of the Society of Genealogists. In subsequent years Tony Foster did much work on updating the Guide. Illness and other problems delayed its completion, but a great incentive at last to complete the new edition was given by Richard Ratcliffe's new introductory booklet *Basic Facts about Quarter Sessions Records*, perhaps the last publication to appear from the F.F.H.S. Publications Company. Fortunately it remains available from the Family History Partnership. Since its publication Richard has kindly made a further check on the complete text of this Guide, adding record office websites and/or email addresses. With these it must always be remembered they are subject to constant change both in content and name. Without the support of Else, Tony and Richard this edition would not have appeared.

As always it is my pleasure to thank the archivists of the county record offices and other repositories in England and Wales for their response and support. Much has been done in the way of cataloguing and listing in recent years. This reflects the continuing dedication of archivists throughout the country to making the records in their charge usable by the researcher.

In many cases excellent guides to individual record offices already exist in print, and it is my hope that references to them here will bring them to readers' attention and increase their use, as well as research in the records of Quarter Sessions themselves. Already some indexing is being done by family history societies. One contributor has commented: 'A great deal of work remains to be done on them. Perhaps as a result of your interest volunteers could be found to undertake some of it'. Such an outcome would in itself justify this Guide and make some recompense for the help given by archivists in its preparation.

J.S.W.G.

BEDFORDSHIRE

Bedfordshire & Luton Archives & Records Service, Bedford.

Q.S. records for the county and some for Bedford borough are listed in the *Guide to the Bedfordshire Record Office*, by Joyce Godber, Beds. C.C., 1957.

There is a Ts calendar of the Sessions Rolls, 1714-1832, extracts only, with personal and place names and subject indexes; unindexed extracts, 1714-1832, are published in *Bedfordshire County Records*, **1**.

Indictment Books, 1651-1660, are published in *Bedfordshire County Records*, **2**. The Society of Genealogists holds an unpublished TS index to Bedfordshire RO compiled by B. J. Gravestock, 1982.

Bedfordshire Licensed Victuallers 1827, published by The EurekA Partnership, 19a Station Road, Stoke Mandeville, Aylesbury, Bucks. HP22 5UL; or see <www.genfair.com>

See also: <archives@bedscc.gov.uk>

County
Sessions rolls, 1714-C20 (gaps 1715, 1717-20, 1723, 1774, 1794-96). To 1837 they are in bound volumes. They include sacrament certificates and oaths of allegiance, removal orders, bastardy papers, examinations and depositions, recognizances, indictments and presentments.

Indictment book, 1651-60 (published).

Sessions minutes, 1711-C20 (gaps 1718-27, 1732, 1762-67).

Calendars of prisoners at Q.S., 1799-1907 (includes Middlesex prisoners, 1863-1879) and Assizes, 1785-1886, 1889-1907.

County Gaol: roll of debtors, 1770-1854; registers of prisoners, 1799-1879. In-house database of entries of prisoners to eventually go on-line.

Land Tax assessments, 1797-1832 (see *LWTA*).

Jury lists from 1780 (selection, 1780-1830, published in Beds. Hist. Record Soc. **4**).

Hearth Tax: see *HT*.

Bedford Borough
Minutes, 1647-1718, 1721-1974 (first vol 1647-1664, published Beds. Hist. Record Soc. **26**).

Rolls, 1750-1836 (incomplete series) and calendars of prisoners, 1829-35, 1846 and 1849. Ts calendar at Beds. R.O.

Apprenticeship records 1614-1843 (Ts index).

Some documents at Beds. R.O. including Sacrament certificates, 1751-1798.

For poll books and electoral registers, see *PB* and *ER*; for records of victuallers, see *VL*.

BERKSHIRE

Berkshire Record Office, Reading.

Finding aids: List of all records; *no* transcripts, calendars; Ts index to Order Book, 1703-1834 (place, subject, not personal names).

See also: <arch@reading.gov.uk>

Some Q.S. records now on-line including:
Q.S. rolls 1811-13, 1821-22, 1823-24.

County
Order book, 1703-49, 1771-74, 1779-1969.

Minute books, 1731-50, 1755-79, 1783-95, 1835-36, 1842-1971.

Sessions rolls, 1734 (part), 1736-1935, 1936 (part).

Recognizances Rolls, 1738-43; Books, 1731-39, 1928-43.

Petition and order rolls, 1737-49, 1752, 1766, 1772-73.

Debtors Rools, 1755.

Few Land Tax assessments (see *LWTA*).

Rolls are arranged by session in years and include jury lists and lists of various officials and calendars of prisoners. Use involves working through session bundles, a long and rather grubby task.

Also at the Berkshire Record Office are Q.S. records (main series), listed but with no further finding aids, for the following boroughs:

Abingdon
Minute books, 1853-79, 1955-69.

Order books, 1880-1954. Oath rolls, 1673-1837.

Recognizances, 1635-1750.

Maidenhead
Sessions books, 1686, 1732-1835.

Rolls, 1804-10. Oath rolls, 1749-1835.

Newbury
Sessions books, 1666-1827, 1836-71.

Sessions rolls, 1836-73, 1874-1947 (incomplete), 1948-69. Oath rolls, 1779-1862.

Reading
Sessions Papers, 1682-91, 1764-1919.

Minute Books, 1836-82 (draft), 1882-1939, 1946-69.

Calendar of Prisoners, 1836-1969.

Wallingford
Sessions books, 1713-1836.

Sessions rolls, 1773-1787. Papers, 1679-1808.

Oath rolls, 1696-1702, 1708-12, 1774-1827.

Windsor
Sessions Minutes, 1657-1663; Books, 1717-1959.

Sessions Rolls, 1761, 1768-69 (filed with county records), 1866-1901.

No significant Q.S. records survive for Hungerford.

For poll books and electoral registers, see *PB* and *ER*; for records of victuallers, see *VL*.

See also *The People of Wallingford* (2 vols.) pub. by The EurekA Partnership (see left under Beds.).

BUCKINGHAMSHIRE

| **Centre for Buckinghamshire Studies, Aylesbury.** |

There is a superb published *Calendar to [Bucks.]*
Sessions Records:
1. 1678-94; **2.** 1694-1705; **3.** 1705-12;
4. 1712-18; **5.** 1718-24; **6.** List of Oath-Takers in 1723
(alphabetical, Quakers and Roman Catholics
separate); **7.** 1724-1730 (incl. lists of JPs and
Sheriffs; register of licensed game keepers, manors
and lords, from 1707). All fully indexed. **8.** 1730-33
(not indexed). Vols. **1 - 7** of the Calendars have been
published on microfiche by Buckinghamshire FHS
[PO Box 403, Aylesbury HP21 7GU].

List of main series at R.O., some papers not finally
classified, but Ms lists available.

Ts abstract of 'Casebooks' (chairman's notes of
cases), 1802-35, indexed; draft summary guide.

See also <archives@buckscc.gov.uk>

County
Sessions rolls 1700-1817, Order Books from 1678-
1959 (published, see above). Incl. particulars of
indictments, presentments of constables, recognizances, calendars of prisoners, registration of
dissenting meeting houses, oaths and sacrament
tests.

Insolvent debtors (1807-46); returns for poor,
Aylesbury Hundred 1803.

Jury lists from 1769-1916 (gaps).

Land Tax Assessments, 1780-1832 (see *LWTA*) pub.
Buckingham Hundred, 1788 (EurekA Partnership).

Other tax lists, 1660-1702 (see *HT*).

Settlements and removals 1678-1712, 1712-1724
pub'd by The EurekA Partnership (right, above).

See also 'The County Treasurers 1678-1889',
Records of Bucks., **16** (1953-60); 'The Archives of the
Treasurers of Bucks. before 1889', *Jnl. Soc.
Archivists*, **1**, 3 (April 1956), both by Julian Cornwall.

Licensed Victuallers' Registers, 1753 [Q/RLv],
1792, and *1827* [Q/R/Lv8], whole county, published
by The EurekA Partnership (right, above).

Victuallers' licences 1753, Burnham and Stoke
Hundreds, *Heritage* (Windsor, Slough & District FHS),
7, 1 (Autumn 1978).

Buckingham Borough *(Bucks. Studies)*
Not very extensive. They include:
Order books, 1598-1607, 1748-1828;
Sessions rolls, 1781-1837, mainly incl. indictments
and recognizances, some bastardy papers from
c.1810 and vagrancy orders from c.1820.

High Wycombe Borough *(Wycombe D.C.)*
Not very active, see *History of High Wycombe*,
L.J. Ashford. Microfiche copy of, Court Leet and
Quarter Sessions Court Book, 1758-1837.

Note. Other boroughs in the county, including
Aylesbury, did not have separate Q.S.

For poll books and electoral registers, see *PB* and
ER; for records of victuallers, see *VL*.

The EurekA Partnership [19a Station Road, Stoke
Mandeville, Aylesbury HP22 5UL; email:
<eureka19@btinternet.com>] publish a series for
various places often including material from QS
records [see <www.genfair.com>].

Published, 'The People of':
Beachampton, Chenies, Chesham, Datchet, Denham,
Hartwell and Stone, Lathbury, Newport Pagnell,
Olney, Princes Risborough, Ravenstone, West
Wycombe, Winchendons, and Wooburn.

CAMBRIDGESHIRE

| **Cambridgeshire Record Office, Cambridge.** |

Until 1965 Cambridgeshire and the Isle of Ely were
separate counties.

Lists for all records, but not fully catalogued.
Calendar for Cambridgeshire Order Books, 1661-72,
1689-96, 1699-1713, 1715-74. Card index to persons
accused, convicted or conviction at petty sessions
reported to quarter sessions, 1660-1883 (to be
continued), personal names only.

See also: <www.cambridgeshire.gov.uk/leisure/
archives/holdings/q-s/quartersessions.wcm>

Cambridgeshire
Sessions rolls or bundles, 1730-1958.
Jurors' books, 1828-34, 1847.
Order Books, 1660-72, 1689-96, 1699-C20.
Oaths registers, 1715-32, 1793-1858.
Recognizance registers, 1661-89, 1694-1757.
Licensed victuallers' recognizance registers, 1728-
1758,1764-1828 (see *VL*).
Estreat registers, 1730-65, 1796-1880.
Land Tax assessments, 1829-32 (and other survivals
listed in *Genealogical Sources in Cambridgeshire*;
see also *LWTA*).
Commissions of the Peace, 1754-1878.
Register of annuities, 1767-1835.
Treasurers' accounts, 1799-1888.
Register of gamekeepers, 1804-1921.

Isle of Ely
Sessions files, 1890, 1893, 1920-65.
Order books, 1801-1965.
Special sessions minutes, 1774-1807, 1823-1845.
Register of charity memorials, 1812-13.
Licensed victuallers' recognizance reg., 1822-1823.
Commissions of the Peace, 1837-78.
Oaths registers, 1830-36, 1895-1931.

The following earlier records are among the dio-
cesan archives in *Cambridge University Library*:
Sessions files, 1607,1617-18,1631-32,1637,1639,1643,
1647, 1650, 1654-66, 1726-28, 1736-58, 1760-75.
Minutes, 1740-47.
Sacrament certificates, 1706-36.
Licensed victuallers' recognizances, 1613, 1622,
1624, 1627, 1653-54, 1656-57, 1660-64, 1755-75.

Cambridgeshire *continued*

Cambridge Borough (at *C.R.O.*)
Files, depositions, examinations etc., 1677, 1795, 1809-35, 1857-68, 1871-76, 1886-88.
Order books, 1733-1847, 1863-1945.
Gaol delivery, 1503.
Commissions of the Peace, 1703-1877.

In general, lists of names occur in oaths registers, jurors' books and licensed victuallers' registers.

See also *Some Sessions of the Peace in Cambridgeshire in the Fourteenth Century, 1340, 1380-83*, by M.M. Taylor, Cambridge Ant. Soc., 1942, based on records in Assize Rolls in T.N.A.

For poll books and electoral registers, see *PB* and *ER*; for records of victuallers see also *VL*.

CHESHIRE

Cheshire and Chester Archives and Local Studies, Chester.

Lists of records 1559-1760 are printed in *Cheshire Quarter Sessions, 1559-1760*, Lancashire and Cheshire Record Society **94**. This volume also includes abstracts of documents, mostly taken from the files.
All records are listed at the R.O. For the Register of dissenting meeting houses, 1689-1853, and the File of death warrants, 1801-1848, there are Ts lists available giving name, date, places and other details.
Cheshire Q.S. books and files, *c.*1557-1818, have been microfilmed by Harvester Press Microform Publications Ltd.
Chetham Society NS **79**. This volume includes a list of J.Ps. 1130-1325.

See also: <www.cheshire.gov.uk>

County
Sessions books from 1559, indexed from 1778.
Sessions files from 1571.
Alehouses: registers of licences, 1743-1758, 1827-1828; alesellers' recognizances, 1629-41, 1749-1828 (see *VL*).
Elections: Poll books, 1741, 1722, 1831, 1837, 1841 (see *PB*).
Land Tax assessments, 1780-1832 (see *LWTA*).
Electoral registers from 1832 (see *ER*).
Gamekeepers: registers, 1711-1949.
Gaol: prisoners and transportation 1726-1747 (odd papers only), 1802-57.
Justices of the Peace: commissions, 1681-1859.
Militia: account of payments to militiamen's families 1760-93; officers' declarations 1778-85, 1809-94.
Nonconformists: register of dissenting meeting houses, 1689-1853; declarations as to articles of religion 1704-1732; returns of meeting houses 1829.
Oaths: rolls of subscribers to various oaths, 1673-1837, incl. Test Oath 1723; sacramental certificates 1741-1827.

Cheshire *continued*

Papists: enrolled rentals and deeds of estates 1715-1759; register and certificates of meeting houses, 1791-1848.

Chester
Sessions files from 1488.
Sessions order books, 1799-1866.
Register of prisoners, 1853-72.
City Gaol and House of Correction records, 1808-1872.
Lists of jurors, 1608-1817.
Licensed victuallers recognizances, 1552-1688, 1736-1825 (see *VL*).
Sacrament certificates, 1673-1789.
Transportation bonds, 1731-75; and contracts, 1764-1775.
Justice of the Peace: commissions, 1836-1970, and declarations, 1860-1901.

Wirral Archives Service, Birkenhead Town Hall.

Birkenhead
Minute books, papers etc., 1882-1971.

See also *Charges to the Grand Jury at Quarter Sessions, 1660-1677, by Sir Peter Leicester*, ed. E.M. Halcross, Chetham Society Series 3, vol. **5**.

For poll books and electoral registers, see *PB* and *ER*; for records of victuallers, see *VL*.

CORNWALL

Cornwall Record Office, Truro.

See: <www.cornwall.gov.uk>

County
Order books from 1737. Ts index to 1737-1746 only, names of justices and cases in which they were concerned, places, occupations by trades and industries, subjects (no other personal names). Record books listed with covering dates but no other cataloguing nor calendaring. *No* Sessions Rolls survive.
Commissions of the Peace, 1757-1950, administration and legal records arising (e.g., highway orders of justices etc.).
Land Tax redemption registers, 1805-12 (with other LT records from 1799, microfilmed, copy at Society of Genealogists; see also *LWTA*).

Helston Borough (at *C.R.O.*)
Sessions rolls, 1743-49, 1786-1791, 1801-1826.
Bills of indictment, 1791-1830.
Depositions, 1747-51, 1776-82.
Recognizances, 1788-1824.
Jury lists and sacrament certificates, late C18-early C19.

Virtually no Q.S. records survive for Falmouth and apparently none for Penzance.

For poll books and electoral registers, see *PB* and *ER*.

CUMBERLAND

Q.S. petitions calendared 1686-1762, indexed 1688-1752.

See also: <www.cumbria.gov.uk/archives>

County

Sessions rolls, 1686-1942 (gaps C17 and early C18). Filed quarterly incl. petitions (which cease *c.*1840), indictments, recognizances.

Minute books, 1667-1971 (gaps 1739, 1748-1753).

Indictment books, 1689-1928 (gaps 1709-1740, 1773-1779, 1787-1794).

Abstract books (indictments), 1747-1864.

Convictions books, 1769-1891 (gap 1773-1798), some indexed.

Recognizance books, 1770-1834 (gap 1772-1779).

Order Books (general), 1696-1734.

Order books (public orders, re. County business and re. more than one person), 1730-1889 (gap 1779).

Order books (private orders, re. individuals), 1734-1777.

Debtors' papers, 1756-1834 (many gaps).

County Treasurer: account books, 1710-1889; vouchers, 1739-1885.

Alehouses: recognizance registers, 1753-72; registers 1822-31 (see also *VL*).

Jurors: jury returns, 1714-1869; freeholders' books, 1720-1822 (gaps in both).

Land Tax: duplicate returns, 1761-1829 (listed; see also *LWTA*).

Religion: Oaths of allegiance, 1696-1702, 1723, 1727-1858; returns of Papists and Papists' estates, 1696-1744; register of Papists' deeds and wills 1727-1777.

Printers: registrations, 1799-1858.

Gamekeepers: lists, 1794-1804 (gaps).

Carlisle (at *Cumbria R.O.*)

Minute books, 1766-1894 (excl. 1835-1873 when Carlisle lost its powers).

Rolls, 1801-1812.

Publicans register, 1822-1832 (see *VL*).

Petitions file, c.1717-1741 (see also County Q.S. rolls).

Sacrament certificate file, 1704-1774 (several gaps).

For poll books and electoral registers, see *PB* and *ER*; for records of victuallers, see *VL*.

DERBYSHIRE

See *Derbyshire Guide to the Record Office*, 2nd edn. 1994 (Derbyshire R.O.).

See also *Calendar of Records of the County of Derby, 1558-1896* (1890-99) and *Three Centuries of Derbyshire Annals* (1890), both by J.C. Cox. These indicate the Q.S. records range, 'but should be used with care... The Calendar is based on C.R. Colvile's summary *Report of the County Record Committee*, 1882, and on Colvile's detailed Ms lists compiled from 1872 onwards.' (County Archivist's report, 1962-73).

Various calendars/lists, late C19 Ms and printed, current Mss. Also indexes as below.

Derbyshire names in miscellaneous lists vol 1, 1798-1821: declarations of allegiance 1821; voluntary contributions 1798; associations for the prosecutions of felons 1798-1801; gamekeepers and gentlemen's licences 1798-1814; Quarter Sessions 1798-1799, published by Derbyshire FHS, 1995. *Three centuries of Derbyshire Annals as illustrated by the records of the Quarter Sessions from Queen Elizabeth to Queen Victoria*, by John Cox.

See <www.derbyshire.gov.uk/leisure/record_office> *and email:* <record.offices@derbyshire.gov.uk>

County

Order books from 1682 (bastardy cases, 1682-1800, indexed).

Fragments of bundles from 1558, in more organised form from 1723 but still incomplete.

Minutes of indictments, 1711-1867.

Jurors lists, 1702-29, 1775-1909, 1918.

Badgers, drovers, swailers, 1714,1729, 1746-72.

Gamekeepers' deputations, 1789-1806, 1817-49.

Licensed victuallers' recognizances, 1753-1827 (see *VL*).

Miscellaneous recognizances registers, 1740-1851.

Registers of Papists' estates & allied papers, 1716-78.

Calendars of prisoners, temp. Eliz (1 item), 1694, 1729/30-1758 (19 items), 1761-1878, 1914-71.

Transportation papers, 1730-1772.

Removal orders, 1710-1865 (indexed).

Cotton mills: returns of apprentices, *c.*1841.

Coroners' claims for expenses (giving victims' names, usually the verdict), 1752-1869 (incomplete; indexed).

Land Tax assessments, 1778-1832 (see *LWTA*).

Electoral registers from 1832 (see *ER*).

All are easy to use and most, very useful for family history, though of little or no use for strict genealogy.

Derby Borough

Minute books, 1628-53, William III period, 1709-40, 1843-71.

Jurors, constables, accused etc. (single sheet per year), 1705, 1715, 1728 (?), 1735, 1739-40, 1743-1744, 1745/6, 1748, 1752, 1754-56, 1758-61.

Index of prisoners 1860-1909.

For poll books and electoral registers, see *PB* and *ER*; for records of victuallers see *VL*.

DEVON

Devon Record Office: Brief Guide, Part 1, contains a short list of the different classes of the County Q.S. records series, of which the following is an even more condensed version. Only a small number of Order Books are indexed and there are no transcripts or published copies. A more detailed catalogue is available in the search room. There is a leaflet on *Crime and Punishment*. A. H. A. Hamilton, *Quarter Sessions from Queen Elizabeth to Queen Anne,* published 1878

See also: <devrec@devon.gov.uk>

County

Court in Session: General
Order books with indexes, 1592-C20.
Estreats, 1718-1863.
Bundles of writs, indictments, court and administration papers, 1592-1971.
Returns of jurymen, 1728-1915.
Grand and petty jury lists (also appeals), 1730-1876.
Lists of freeholders, 1711-1807.
Recognizance books, 1730 -1881.
Process books, 1693-1765.
Convictions register and index, 1753-83.
Registers of appeals (also jury lists), 1730-1876.
Registers of convictions for swearing (also register of badgers), 1729-66.
Constables' presentments, 1679, 1685, 1726, 1768.

Court in Session: Oaths
Rolls of oaths of Allegiance etc., 1674-1827, registers, 1827-1880.
Oaths of Abhorrence, 1665-1685.
Association to protect William III, 1696 (see *HT*).
Sacrament certificates, 1688-1828.
Papists' oaths, 1791-1803.
Dissenting ministers' oaths, 1780-1825.
Dissenting teachers' subscriptions, 1760-1776.
Commissions to take Justices' oaths, 1667, 1732-1874.
Commissions of Peace, 1643-1878.

Court in Session: Gaol and Debtors
Gaol calendars, 1665-1810, 1842-1953; (Assizes) 1854-1919.
Register of insolvent debtors, 1817-47.
Debtors' papers, 1769-1844.

Documents Deposited and Registered
Register of badgers (itinerant hawkers) licences, 1729-1779.
Licences, alehouses (licensed victuallers) returns, 1607-1821; and recognizances, 1822-28; registers 1753-84, 1822-1827 (see *VL*).
Religion: registration of Papists' estates, 1717-1776; recognizances of butchers not to sell meat in Lent, 1627-1661.
Maimed soldiers' petitions for annuities, 1660-1695.
Transportation of felons (bonds and contracts), 1726-1776.

Taxation: Hearth Tax papers 1662-1688 (see *HT*); Land Tax assessments, 1747, 1751, 1780-1832 (see *LWTA*).

Note: The foregoing is only a fairly arbitrary selection from the *Brief Guide*, which also lists many other classes of record that might be of use to family historians; also it indicates the number of volumes, bundles etc.

In addition to the County series, as listed in the Brief Guide and above, the **Devon R.O.** holds records for the separate sessions for the City of **Exeter** and Boroughs of **Dartmouth** and **Tiverton**.
For **Barnstaple, Bideford, Great Torrington** and **South Molton**, see *North Devon R.O.*
For **Plymouth**, see *Plymouth & West Devon R.O.*

Exeter
Court in Session (volumes)
Minute books, 1618-1872.
Order books, 1866-1971.
Recognizance books, 1709-1917.
Presentments of nuisances, 1550-1657.
Transportation of felons papers, 1719-1789.

Court in Session (loose files)
Session rolls (i.e., bundles of writs, indictments, jury lists etc.), 1557-1700.
Summary convictions, C18-C20.
Recognizances, 1615-1911.
Grand Jury presentments, 1671-1829.
Sworn informations, 1702-1769 (detailed list including personal names).
Indictments, 1611-1865.
Oaths of allegiance etc, 1698-1753, 1829-1858.
Sacrament certificates, 1673-1826 (index in search room).
Gaol calendars, 1631-1916.
Gaol sentence books, 1801-1863.
Registers of badgers, 1740-1771.
Victuallers' recognizances, 1758-1799 (see *VL*).
Returns of Meeting Houses, 1812-1831.
Registration of Papists' estates, 1717-1731.

Hearth Tax, 1671-74 (see *HT*).

Tiverton Borough
Minute books, 1740-1813.

Dartmouth Borough
C18-C19 documents filed in chronological order.

Barnstaple Borough
Court books, 1581-1835
Sessions rolls, 1711-1774.
Presentments, 1590, 1674-80, 1717-1770.
Writs, declarations, depositions etc., mixed with mayor's court papers, 16th-18th cent.

Bideford Borough
Order books,1659-1707, 1715-75, 1787-1818, 1820-1888.
Prison register, 1838-1852.

Devon *(N.D.R.O.) continued*

Great Torrington Borough
Order books, 1686-1835.

South Molton Borough

Order books,1671-1703, 1705-47, 1756-75.
Alehouse recognizances, 1753-79 (see *VL*).

Plymouth & West Devon Record Office, Plymouth.

Q.S. records for **City of Plymouth** (but not Devonport or Stonehouse: see County) leaflet issued; see also *Calendar of the Plymouth Municipal Records*, R.N. Worth (1893) and *A Guide to the Archives Dept. of Plymouth City Libraries*, Part 1, E. Welch (1962).

The records are patchy, no Sessions Rolls survive, and Order Books before 1772 contain many administrative matters.

See also: <www.plymouth.gov.uk/archives>

City of Plymouth
Order books, 1675-94, 1704-1808.
Transubstantiation declarations 1730-42.
Lists of victualling houses, 1802-24 (see *VL*).
Calendars of prisoners, 1805-26.
Writ books, 1620-1837.
Estreat books, 1783-1819.

Order books and other records between 1816 and 1941 were destroyed by enemy action.

For poll books and electoral registers, see *PB* and *ER*; for records of victuallers see *VL*.

DORSET

Dorset History Centre, Dorchester.

See *Index to County Records*, by A.C. Cox, 1938 (actually a list, not an index).

See also: <www.dorsetforyou.com/archives> and email: <archives@dorsetcc.gov.uk>

County
Order books, 1625-38 (for publication by Dorset Record Society), 1663-74, 1686-1951 (with contemporary indexes from 1754, of limited usefulness).
Clerk of the Peace's minutes, 1669-87, 1701-99, 1858-89.
Plea books, 1682-93, 1700-1810.
Rolls/files, 1709-1970 (a few odd gaps; some categories in separate series).
Calendar of prisoners, 1801-1970.

Miscellaneous records include:
List of jurors, 1719-91, 1825-1922 (with several small gaps).
Alehouse recognizance registers, 1714-1770 (some small gaps) (see *VL*).
Land Tax assessments, 1780-1832 (see *LWTA*).
Marriage Tax: Lyme Regis, 1695-1703; Colway, 1695 (see *HT*).

Boroughs (at *Dorset H.C.*)

Bridport
Indictments, etc., 1635-1640.
Alehouse keepers' bonds, 1581-1604 (see *VL*).

Dorchester
Minutes, 1676-1723.
Sessions books, 1676-1827.
Rolls, 1689-1831 (odd years missing).
Justices' qualification rolls, 1724-55, 1771-1834, 1824-66.
Alehouse recognizance registers, 1795-1828 (see *VL*).

Lyme Regis
Court books, 1647-1723/4 (with odd gaps) (calendared), 1738-1835 (indexed).
Rolls,1578-1598, 1600-1835.
Recognizances, 1598-1612, 1672-1692, 1695-1726, 1734-1790, 1803-1830.
Jury lists, 1622, 1694-1725, 1733-99, 1820-1823, 1829-1835.
Presentments of grand inquest and constables, 1664, 1669, 1685-88, 1694-1710, 1714-27, 1732-80, 1784-1835.
Alehouse recognizances and lists, 1605, 1613-14, 1625, 1694/5-1709, 1718, 1735-80, 1784-1827 (see *VL*).
Oaths certificates etc., 1653-1835.

Dorset *(D.R.O.)continued*

Poole

Sessions books, 1678-1699, 1840-1957.
Rolls of Oaths of Allegiance, 1702-11, 1714-17, 1722-1723, 1726-27, 1756-1809, 1830.
Sacrament certificates, 1700-1830.
Jury lists, 1656, 1701, 1708, 1713, 1725-29, 1736-1823.
Presentments (public nuisances), 1656, 1680, 1692, 1700-10, 1712-1835.
Indictments, 1623, 1656, 1701-02, 1706-09, 1711-12, 1736-51, 1754-60, 1762-1807, 1835.
Felonies, 1785-1833.
Recognizances, 1622-23, 1629, 1631-32, 1634, 1637, 1655-56, 1701, 1704, 1706-08, 1711-13, 1731-1840.
Warrants, 1629, 1632, 1679-82, 1702, 1725-30, 1739-42, 1744, 1776-77, 1779-80, 1787, 1790, 1792-96, 1801-02, 1804-05, 1807, 1811-29, 1831, 1833, 1837.
Alehouse recognizances, 1786-1830.
Theatre licences, 1790, 1808, 1810, 1812, 1814-15, 1818, 1828-31, 1833-35.

Wareham Borough

Court of Record Books, 1721-94, 1821-67.
Oath of Allegiance, 1761-66.
Election and Admission of Officials, 1721-1881.

Weymouth Museum, Weymouth.

Weymouth and Melcombe Regis

Minutes of presentations, recognizances, indictments, and some examinations/depositions, 1616-83.
Examinations/depositions, 1699-1729.
Minutes of the Borough Quarter Sessions summarizing court business, 1762-99.
Precept with jury lists, 1768-1801.
Original indictments, 1771-1835.

For poll books and electoral registers, see *PB* and *ER*; for records of victuallers, see *VL*.

Co. DURHAM

Early Q.S. records for the county are published in *Durham Q.S. Rolls 1471-1625*, ed. and cal. by C.M. Fraser, Surtees Society **199**, 1991. The actual years covered are 1471-73, 1510-12, 1545-46 [The National Archives]; 1555-57 [Durham University Library]; and 1596-1625 [Durham C.R.O.].

Durham County Record Office, Durham.

There is a detailed catalogue of the Q.S. material in the searchroom, with a condensed description in the Record Office *Handlist* **4**. Detailed catalogue of Quarter Sessions records also available on the Office's website at:
<www.durham.gov.uk/recordoffice>

Co. Durham *continued*

County

Process records
Indictment rolls, 1596-1636 (published to 1625; missing, 1614, 1619-21, 1623, 1630, 1633), 1661-1756 (missing, 1663, 1666-67, 1682, 1695, 1700-1703, 1706-10, 1715-17, 1720, 1722-23, 1726-27, 1730-33, 1737-41, 1744-46, 1748-49, 1753, 1755), 1780, 1808, 1812, 1823, 1840-1968; indexes, 1880-1926.
Order books, 1616-44, 1649-56, 1660-82, 1686-1971.
Rough order books, 1735-36, 1738-1746, 1750-56, 1774-1880.
Process books, 1619-1636, 1735-1752, 1764-1778.
Calendars of prisoners, 1867-1966.
Recognizances, 1855, 1875-1949.
Petitions etc, 1746-1905 (major gaps).

Administration
Militia family relief payments, 1807-11.

Enrolled records
Returns of jurors, 1766, 1796, 1908.
Victuallers' recognizances, 1716-18; returns of alehouse keepers, 1783-86, 1804 (see *VL*).
Gamekeepers' deputations, 1802-07, 1825-83.
Registers of Roman Catholic estates, 1717-1790.
Fines for non-attendance at church, 1607, 1829.
Certificates of Roman Catholic chapels and priests, 1791-1854; nonconformist meeting houses, 1829.

Deposit and Registration
Land Tax assessments, 1759-61, 1780s-1830 (with gaps) (see *LWTA*).
Land Tax redemptions, 1798-1813.
Commissioners of Land Tax, 1780-81.
Inhabited house tax, 1796; returns of farmers near the sea coast, 1796.
Electoral registers, 1833-92 (see *ER*).

Durham University Library Archives and Special Collections.

County
Rolls, 1555-1557. Published.
Land Tax assessments, C18-19 (see *LWTA*).

Tyne and Wear Archives Service,
Newcastle upon Tyne.

See *User Guide* **14**, *Court and Police Records* (available free, s.a.e. required).

See also: <www.tyneandweararchives.org.uk>

Sunderland
Order books, 1907-1944.
Draft order books, 1907-49, 1963-66.

The National Archives, Kew, London.

Rolls, 1471-73 [Durham 19/1/1], 1510-12 [Durham 3/75], 1545-46 [Durham 13/265]. Published.

For poll books and electoral registers, see *PB* and *ER*; for records of victuallers, see *VL*.

ESSEX

Essex Record Office, Chelmsford.

The Q.S. records for the County are listed and described in some detail in the *Guide to the Essex Record Office*, 2nd edn., 1969, by F.G. Emmison, which is essential reading though now o.p.

There is a Ts calendar, which appears on the RO's website <www.ero.enquiry@essexcc.gov.uk> *and email:* <ero.enquiry@essexcc.gov.uk> 1556-1714, to all documents in the Sessions Rolls, with index of parishes and bridges. Personal names are indexed with volumes for 1556-1590.

The first Order Book, 1652-1661, with indexes of persons, places and subjects, is published as vol. **1** of the Essex Edited Texts, Essex R.O., 1973.

County

The Court in Session
Sessions rolls, 1556-C20 (incomplete 1557-63, 1670-90, otherwise an almost complete series from 1564); and
Sessions Bundles, an independent parallel series, from early C17.
After 1694 the Rolls are largely confined to formal parchment documents, and papers are in the enlarged series of Sessions Bundles, 1694-1921. Together they include (for the whole period unless shown otherwise):
Presentments;
Indictments;
Informations (trade offences), 1591-1645;
Summary convictions, 1584-1849; alphabetically arranged registers, 1791-1860;
Recognizances (to appear at sessions);
Recognizances of licensed victuallers (see *VL*);
Jury lists and panels;
Calendars of prisoners, 1582-1842; also printed calendars, 1860-1908;
Maintenance orders, 1576-1687;
Petitions (few after 1750);
Sacrament certificates, 1673, 1676-1827;
Presentments of recusants, 1641;
Presentments of alehouses, 1644 (see *VL*);
Removal orders of paupers;
Dissenting Meeting House certificates, from 1695-c.1730; register 1761-1852.

Process and Cognate records
Plea and Process Rolls, 1602-33, 1714-78.
'Pye Lists of Writs', 1650-1654.
Process books, 1681-94, 1709-1918 (with index of defendants in each of 31 vols.).
Estreats of Fines, 1627-49, 1726-1914 (incl. lists of recusants 1641-42).
Sessions Books, 1632-43, 1686-87, 1718-C20 (Minute books, incl. recognizances except for alehouses, parties, abode, occupation from mid-C18 etc.).
Order books, 1652-61 (published), 1671-86, 1698-C20.

Essex (County) *continued*

Enrolment, registration and deposit
Religion: Registers of Declarations against Transubstantiation, 1673; Sacrament certificates, 1673, 1676-1710; Association rolls, 1696; Oaths of Allegiance etc., 1689-1882; Papists' oaths, 1778-1815.
Papists' estates, 1717-86 (calendar, personal name and parish index).
Taxation: Hearth Tax, 1662 (index of personal names); 1668; 1671-73 (see *HT*).
Land Tax assessments, 1780-1832, with index to all personal names, 1782 only (see *LWTA*).
Electors' lists and registers, 1832-88 (see *ER*).
Poll books, 1810, 1812, 1830, 1831, 1832, 1835, 1836, 1837, 1841; index to all names in poll books, 1810 (see *PB*).
Deputations to gamekeepers, registers, 1711-1907. Index of lords of manors.
Vagrants' passes and examinations, 1779-1835 (arranged alphabetically by names of vagrants' 1779-90, 1791-1810, in annual bundles within each letter group).
Licensed tradesmen: victuallers' and alehouse keepers' original recognizances, 1580-1612, 1640, 1712 (these are additional to those on the Sessions Rolls); annual registers, 1769-1828 (complete except for 1771) (index of licensees' names) (see *VL*).
Badgers and other dealers: registers of recognizances, 1733, 1759-70 (with index of licensees' names).
Jurors: lists (freeholders' books), 1734 (published), 1759, 1763-83, 1815, with indexes of all names, 1734 and 1759.

Liberty of Havering-atte-Bower
Sessions files, 1771-1892.
Sessions court or minute books, 1730-1803, 1835-1892.

Borough of Colchester
See H. Harrod, *Repertory of records and evidences of the Borough of Colchester* (1865), pp. 14-17, 28-31. There are no names indexes, contemporary or modern, to these records. The Office has recently compiled a catalogue which takes into account corrections and recent accessions.

Sessions and gaol delivery rolls, 1561-1672, 1687 (jury only), 1690-94, 1698-1740, 1764-1814 (incl. oath rolls 1764-1810).
Sessions rolls and files (often with filed miscellaneous papers), 1516, 1583, 1598, 1618, 1629, 1654-55, 1673, 1689-1861, 1955, 1957-71.
Sessions papers, calendars, certificates, indentures, depositions etc., 1738-77, 1783-1820, 1825-49.
Sessions books, 1599-1603, 1630-63, 1693-1822.
Sessions minute books, 1734-41, 1764-1826, 1836-77, 1895-1971.
Examinations and recognizances, 1561-1687.
Alehouse keepers' recognizances, 1647-1672, 1765-1819 (see *VL*).

Essex (E.R.O., Chelmsford) *continued*

Borough of Maldon
Q.S. memoranda, 1696-1744, and Record Books, 1811-82; other "Court' material C14-C19, including Court of Record, enrolment of apprenticeship indentures etc., 1565-1869.

Borough of Saffron Walden
Court books, Q.S., 1657-1900, on microfilm at Essex R.O. Original records remain with *Town Clerk, Saffron Walden Town Council, 18 High Street, Saffron Walden CB10 1EH.*

Harwich Town Council,
Guildhall, Church Street, Harwich CO12 3DS.

Borough of Harwich
See *Calendar of Muniments of Borough of Harwich* (Harwich Corporation, 1931). The records appear to have been in haphazard bundles, and thus are listed in very confused order. The 'Key to Sessions Records' (p. 17) and index entries are unreliable and a detailed search of the Calendar is recommended. The following are a selection only of records that may be relevant.

Sessions books, *c.*1600-1836.
Sessions papers, early C17-1757.
Jury list, 1621.
Records of sessions, 1670-84; verdicts of Grand Juries with signatures, early C18; cases, 1657-1687.
Oaths of Allegiance and Supremacy, 1696-1767, 1799-1836.
True bills, 1711-1768.
Presentments, 1793-95.
Recognizances, 1793-96, 1800, 1807.
Sacrament certificates, 1696-1723, 1743-89 (gaps).

Centre for Kentish Studies, Maidstone.

Licensed victuallers' recognizances, 1636-1807, amongst Sandwich Q.S. records include a few for Brightlingsea.
For poll books and electoral registers, see *PB* and *ER*; for records of victuallers, see *VL*.

GLOUCESTERSHIRE and BRISTOL

Gloucestershire Record Office, Gloucester.

Q.S. records for the County and for the Borough of Tewkesbury are described in some detail in *Gloucestershire Q.S. Archives, 1669-1889...*, Glos. C.C., 1958; and in *Handlist of the Contents of the Gloucestershire Record Office*, 2nd edition, 1979. This gives brief details of all the Office's holdings.

There are few finding aids, but there is a Ts calendar showing the contents of the Order Rolls for every fifth year, 1735-1840. Enrolled Summary Convictions [Q/PC 2] are being calendared by Mrs I. Wyatt, and at present run from October 1781 to September 1837.

See also: <www.gloucestershire.gov.uk/archives> *and email:* <archives@gloucestershire.gov.uk>

County
Order rolls, 1728-1880 (incl. grand jury presentments; very numerous poor law settlement removal orders; depositions *c.*1770-1812; sacrament certificates *c.*1800-1838; petitions, incl. petitions for dissenters' meeting houses; calendars, described above).
Depositions, 1727-70, 1834-1971.
Indictments, 1728-1971.
Indictment books, 1660-68/9 (with contemporary index); 1770-73, 1808-1910 (with contemporary indexes).
Process books, 1745-1769.
Prisoners: Gaol calendars, 1728-1889; indexed 1728-1789 and 1815-1825; references to the gaol calendars are included in *Transportees from Gloucestershire to Australia 1783-1842*, ed. Irene Wyatt, 1988.
Jury panels, 1687/8; lists and books, 1728-1878.
Minute books, 1781-1965.
Order books, 1672-1692, 1702-1868.
Land Tax assessments, 1775-1832 (see *LWTA*).

City of Gloucester
Sessions rolls from 1690.
Order books, 1698/9-1701 and 1759-1812.
Minute books, 1773-1792.
Indictment books, 1638/9-1684/5.
Alehouse licences, 1674-1836 (see *VL*).

Borough of Tewkesbury
Order books, 1774-1946.
Few other Q.S. records pre mid-C19.

For Bristol, see page 14.

Gloucestershire and Bristol *continued*

BRISTOL

Bristol Record Office, *Bristol.*

See *Guide to the Bristol Archives Office*, by E. Ralph, 1971.
All the records are listed.
Sessions papers are not complete. Partial transcripts of some of these (for 1753, 1760-67) have been published in *Notes on Bristol History*, *9*, by the Department of Extra-Mural Studies, University of Bristol, 1971. Transcription is an on-going project, with some years between 1753 and 1808 completely or partially covered, unpublished but easily consulted at the Record Office.
Bristol Gaol Delivery Fiats, 1741-1799, have been published in Bristol Record Society, **11**, 1989.
List of Prisoners tried at Quarter Sessions between April 1816 and Jan 1837 with sentences. Sentences of the prisoners who were tried ... at the Quarter Sessions for the City of Bristol held January (October) 1836 (July, 1837, October, 1841, July 1843),

See also: <www.bristol.gov.uk>
and email: <archives.bristol-city.gov.uk>

Bristol
Sessions minute books, 1595-1705.
Doggett or record books, 1682-1753, 1808-1958.
Papers, 1708-1839 (comprising informations, examinations, presentments, jury lists, calendars of prisoners, petitions, removal orders, bankruptcy papers, sacrament certificates etc.; see note on transcripts above).
Files from 1824.
Convictions, 1695-1795.
Recognizances, 1673-1809.
Presentments (by constables), 1676-1700.
Jury books, 1731-42, 1905-1958.
Alehouse keepers' licences, 1654-1814; register of inn-keepers and vintners, 1802-1811 (see *VL*).

Note. Bristol had its own Assize jurisdiction up to 1831 and did not form part of the Western Assize Circuit; the Mayor was a justice of oyer and terminer and general gaol delivery, these records being found amongst those of the Sessions.

For poll books and electoral registers, see *PB* and *ER*; for records of victuallers, see *VL*.

HAMPSHIRE

Hampshire Record Office, *Winchester.*

A short guide to *Quarter Sessions Records in the Hampshire Record Office*, by Philippa White, 1990, is available from the Office, £1.00 + 50p p&p.
Ms notebooks by J.S. Furley on early Q.S. records, 1559-1716 (not very legible). Some subject indexes, but notes rarely include names, except Justices and Grand Jurymen, 1679-91 (indexed), and names of Papists, 1657 (Indictments and Presentments, 1646-1660).

Hampshire *continued*

Subject card index to C19 Order Books (no personal names).
J.S. Furley, *Quarter Session government in Hampshire in the 17th century*, Winchester, Watson & Sons, nd. N. R. Webb, *A calendar of the prisoners in the new prison or County Brideswell near the city of Winchester for the Easter sessions, to be holden at the Castle of the said city on Monday April 16, 1798*. A. McGowan, *The Winchester confessions 1615-1616: depositions of travellers, gipsies, fraudsters & makers of counterfeit documents including a vocabulary of the Romany language*, published by Romany & Travellers FHS, 1996.

See also:
<hants.gov.uk/record-office/local_gov/quarter.html>

County
Minutes of Sessions of Peace and Gaol Delivery, 1559-1577.
Minute books, 1624-34, 1679-1813.
Book of recognizances, 1607-1627.
Order books, 1607-1967.
Sessions rolls, 1658, 1678-1972 (not all survive for every year).
Oaths and Declarations, 1679-1971; Sacrament Certificates, 1683-1829.
Registration of Papists' Estates, 1717-1775.
Land Tax assessments, 1800-1832 (see *LWTA*).

Of the above, Calendars of Prisoners (in Sessions Rolls) and Land Tax assessments would be the most useful to family historians.
See also *Quarter Sessions Government in Hampshire in 17th Century*, by J.S. Furley (Winchester, n.d.).

There were separate Q.S. (records at **Hampshire R.O.** except for Southampton and Portsmouth) for:

Winchester
Order books, 1660-1787.
Minute books, 1714-1957.
Sessions papers, 1510-1971.

Andover
Minute books, 1899-1971.
Proceedings, 1931-1957.
Informations, examinations and presentments, 1649-1653, 1719-1801, 1818.

Basingstoke
Sessions rolls, 1642, 1652-64, 1688-99, 1700-1836.
Examinations, 1653-1663, 1687-1718.
Minute book, 1823-1836.

Romsey
Book of proceedings, 1820-36.

Dorset History Centre, *Dorchester.*

Bournemouth
Minutes, 1899-1971.
Indictments, 1899-1911.
After-trial calendars of prisoners, 1899-1971.

Hampshire *continued*

Portsmouth City Museum and Records Service.

See <www.portsmouthrecordoffice.co.uk>

Portsmouth

Sessions were held twice yearly rather than quarterly.

Sessions files, 1652-1781 (occasional gaps), consisting mainly of depositions, informations, recognizances, examinations, jury summonses etc..
Sessions books, 1785-1831 (containing calendars, jury lists etc.).
Indictments, 1848-1869. Oath rolls, 1673-1858.
Sacrament certificates, 1673-1782.

Publications: *Borough Sessions Papers, 1653-1688*, A.J. Willis and Margaret J. Hoad (1971); *Book of Original Entries, 1731-1751*, ed. N.W. Surry and J.H. Thomas (1976; both Portsmouth Record Series). *Records of the City of Portsmouth, 1835-1965*, 6 vols.

Southampton Archives Services.

Southampton

The Q.S. records are described briefly in *Southampton Records, 1*, a guide to Corporation Records, 1964 (60p + p&p). The Office has Ts lists of Sessions Rolls, Sessions Books and Examination Books; calendar of 945+ miscellaneous loose papers, 1682-1840; rough lists for 390 Sacrament Certificates, by name 1665-1816; and 106 Grand Jury presentments, by year, 1686-1789.

See: <www.southampton.gov.uk/leisure/archives> *and email:* <city.archives@southampton.gov.uk>

Sessions rolls, 1622, 1632, 1642-1842 (many gaps; later rolls destroyed by enemy action).
Sessions books: Order books, 1609-35, 1694-97, 1730-66; draft order book, 1823-26; Highways sessions books, 1693-97, 1774-1837; highway rate books, 1756-66; recognizance book, 1632-48; register of alehouse keepers, 1661-68 (see *VL*); registers of apprentices, 1609-1740 (published in Southampton Record Series **12**, A.J. Willis and A.L. Merson, 1968).
Examination Books (published in *Books of Examinations and Depositions, 1570-1594*, G.H. Hamilton (1914)): incl. Books of Remembrance, 1576-77; *Books of Examinations, 1590-94; also Books of Examinations, 1601, 1602, 1622-44*, R.C. Anderson (1926-36).
Books of Remembrance, 1575, 1578-79, 1583-87; Books of Examinations, 1648-1698 (unpublished).
Hearth Tax, 1662; other tax assessments 1664-99 (*HT*).

Sessions papers include Sacrament Certificates, 1665-1816; lists of jurors 1778-89, 1835; lists of licensed victuallers, 1829-1835 (see *VL*).

Assize of Bread: the earliest volume (part of the first book of remembrance) is printed in *The Assize of Bread Book, 1477-1517*, R.C. Anderson (1923). Later unpublished volumes, 1558-1579, 1596-1602.

Isle of Wight County Record Office, *Newport.*

See <record.office@iow.gov.uk>

Newport Borough

Alehouse licences, 1730-52.
Certificates of convictions, 1734-1833.
Corn returns, c1706-c1826.
Estreats, c1742-c1834.
Grand Jury presentations, 1811-36.
Indictments, 1768-1836.
Minute books, 1654-1836.
Jurors & other office holders, c1700-40's.
Oaths & declarations, 1716-1864.
Recognizances, c1577-1869.
Sacrament certificates, 1673-1827.

For poll books and electoral registers, see *PB* and *ER*; for records of victuallers, see *VL*.

HEREFORDSHIRE

Herefordshire Record Office, *Hereford.*

A printed handlist of the Q.S. records for the **County** and for the **City of Hereford** is available. There are no indexes.

A. J. Camp, *List of persons transported from Hertfordshire to America 1646-1774 extracted from Quarter Session Records* [typescript] 1959.

See also: <archives@herefordshire.gov.uk>

County

Order books from 1674-1971.
Rolls, files, arranged chronologically, 1697-1971.
Calendars of prisoners, 1802-1971 (convictions, 1814-93, microfilmed, copy at SoG).
Land Tax returns, c.1780-1830 (see *LWTA*).

City of Hereford

Earliest survival date 1475, but early files very mixed.

Borough of Leominster

Few records survive.

For poll books and electoral registers, see *PB* and *ER*; for records of victuallers, see *VL*.

HERTFORDSHIRE

Hertfordshire Archives & Local Studies, *Hertford.*

The Q.S. records of Hertfordshire are well served with finding aids. They are described in the *Guide to the Hertfordshire Record Office*, Part 1 (Herts. C.C., 1961), and extracts from the sessions records, with indexes and appendices, are published in *Hertfordshire County Records*, 10 vols. (H.C.C. 1905-1957).

See also: <www.hertfordshire.org/libsleisure/heritage/HALS>

N.B. HALS has a minimum charge of £7.00 for enquiries and requests by phone, post, fax or e-mail.

Hertfordshire (HA&LS) *continued*

Note. The Liberty of St. Albans covered nearly a quarter of the county, and is distinct from the Borough.

Sessions Rolls 1588-1894 (vols. **1-3**);
Sessions Records: Liberty of St. Albans 1770-1840 (**4**);
Sessions Books 1619-1843 (vols. **5-10**).

There are also unpublished aids:
Calendar of Liberty sessions records, 1841-1874;
Complete calendar of County sessions rolls which were formerly at Hatfield House, 1588-1619;
List of Hertford Borough Records, R.T. Andrews, 1913;
List of Borough of St. Albans records, W. Le Hardy,;
List of landlords' names taken from County and Liberty victuallers' recognizances (see *VL*).

County and Liberty of St. Albans
County Q.S. rolls from 1588 (gaps, 1618-19, 1621, 1623-24, 1627-38, 1642, 1645, 1648, 1651, 1737).
Liberty Q.S. rolls, 1784-1874.

There are many gaps in other series of records and details can be found in the published guide. Hertford Borough rolls are no longer in their original state so gaps cannot be easily defined. Q.S. books for the Liberty jurisdiction also include details of St. Albans Borough Sessions, 1758-1814.
The published guide gives details of the types of records available for the County (C) and Liberty (L) jurisdictions.

Records of use to family historians containing lists of names include:

Registers of badgers, drovers and tradesmen, C 1686-1710, 1765-67; L 1770-72; gamekeepers, C 1711-1859; L 1764-1868; printers, C 1799-1868;
Victuallers' recognizances: C 1817-28; L 1786-1825; Hertford Borough 1623-1828 (see *VL*);
Commissions of the Peace: C 1588-1613, 1705-1840, 1878-1954; L 1723-1856;
Lists of Justices: C 1820-61; L 1819-61;
Oath Rolls: Dissenters, C 1689-1831; L 1780-1811; Justices, C 1761-1867, L 1831-38, 1859-75; Oaths of Allegiance, C 1696-1836, L 1776-1858; Hertford Borough Declarations and various oaths, 1653-1780;
Sacrament certificates: C 1702-1828; L 1784- 1858; Hertford Borough 1680-1828;
Jurors lists: C 1728-1920; L 1842, 1874-88; Hertford Borough 1589-1616, 1627-1740;
Poll Books: C 1697, 1714-1805; Borough of St. Albans 1818; Borough of Hertford poll books and lists of freemen since 1625 to 1839 (see *PB*);
Voters lists: C 1832-1915, 1918-32 (with gaps), 1915 to date (see *ER*);
Land Tax assessments: whole county, 1711-67, 1780-1832 (see *LWTA*).

Borough of Hertford
Q.S. records survive for the period 1573-1858. These incl. jury panels, indictments, recognizances, examinations, petitions, informations, certificates, lists of licensees and vagrants, declarations and oaths.

St. Albans Borough
Sessions Rolls, 1784-1820, include jury lists, gaol and House of Correction calendars, sacrament certificates, Informations and Complaints etc., recognizances, and accounts. A Calendar, ed. David Dean, is published in Hertfordshire Record Society, **7**, 1991. Introduction lists supplementary sources. Indexed, but does not generally include names of jurors, vagrants and sureties. Full transcripts (not indexed), compiled by members of the local Architectural and Archaeological Society, are available at the St. Albans Library. Systematic searching of the rolls is both difficult and time consuming since they are still in their tightly rolled condition.
Some early minute books etc. were shared with the Liberty and these are at the Hertfordshire Archives and Local Studies.

HUNTINGDONSHIRE
(now part of Cambridgeshire)

County
The Q.S. records for Huntingdonshire are few, especially before 1780, but some early material survives in the British Library. Records are more numerous thereafter but not in any quantity until 1815.

British Library Manuscripts Collection.

Writs, recognizances etc., 1559-1602 [Add. Mss. 39433-51]; 1559 [39243]; 1560 [39216]; 1569 [39390]; 1571 [39249, 39585]; 1577 [39579]; 1578 [39250, 39391]; 1580 [39080]; 1583 [39084, 39261]; 1586 [39371]; 1587 [39128, 39158, 39253]; 1588 [39254]; 1597 [39096, 39306]; 1599 [39309]; 1600 [39160, 39326]; 1614 [39262]; 1643 [39093].
Rolls, Oaths of Supremacy and Allegiance, 1673-86 [Add. Mss. 27353].

County Record Office (Cambs. C.C., Huntingdon branch), Huntingdon.

There is a Ts list of Q.S. papers, 1734-1860 (copies also at C.R.O., Cambridge, and at National Register of Archives, London); a card index of names in settlement papers 1764-1842; and the Land Tax years are listed in *Genealogical Sources in Cambridgeshire*, J.M. Farrar (Cambs. C.C.).

See also: <Cambridgeshire.gov.uk/leisure/archives>

Papers, originally arranged by session, 1734-1971.
Minute books, 1782-1808, 1816-1965.
Recognizance register, 1835-1842.
Oath books, 1837-1929.
Annuitants, 1752-1807; freeholders, c.1767-c.1807 [in Hinchinbrooke MSS].
Parish settlement papers, 1764-1842.
Land Tax assessments, 1767, 1805-32 (see *LWTA*).

Huntingdon Borough
Minute books, 1765-68, 1776, 1788-1836.
Papers, 1812, 1823-36.

For poll books and electoral registers, see *PB* and *ER*; for records of victuallers, see *VL*.

KENT

| **Centre for Kentish Studies**, *Maidstone.* |

See also: <www.kent.gov.uk/archives>
and email: <archives@kent.co.uk>

The Q.S. records for the County (for East Kent sessions held at Canterbury, and West Kent sessions held at Maidstone), and boroughs except for Canterbury, are very fully described in the excellent *Guide to the Kent County Archives Office*, Felix Hull, Kent C.C., 1958, and supplements.

The Kent FHS has published microfiche of finding aids to QS records:

Catalogue of County holdings [MF 650-657].

Calendar of County Sessions papers 1596-1605, from rare printed book [MF 466].

Calendars of County Sessions papers, 1574-1622 [MF 468-469], 1639-1677 [MF 467]; 1639-40, 1650-52 [MF 1653], 1653-71 [MF 1655], 1686-1715 [MF 1654].

Index of persons (24,000 names) 1596-1605, 1574-1622, 1639-1677, by Peter Manning, 18 Stratford Avenue, Rainham, Kent ME8 0EP. Searches £2 per surname.

City/Borough of Canterbury, full calendar, 1751-1759 (many items *in extenso*) and index (by Duncan Harrington) [MF 164].

See also *Kent at Law 1602*, Louis A. Knafla, HMSO, 1994. This is the first in a series of abstracts of *all* court cases in *all* courts in Kent, mostly from QS records.

L.E.W. Cole, *Index of assizes, quarter sessions and petty sessions (part 1) for 6 parishes near Westesham and Edenbridge, Kent 1560-1750.* microfiche published by North West Kent FHS.

Peter Manning, *Calender of early Quarter Sessions rolls 1596-1606; Calender of Quarter Session records – East Kent order books 1653-4-1671/2; Calender of Quarter Session records – session papers 1639-1677; Calender of Quarter Session records – session papers 1686-1714; Calender of Quarter Session records 1574-1622.*

County

Early judicial records
Sessions rolls, 1600-04.
Gaol delivery roll, 1596-1605.
Recognizances, 1588-1618.
Other records, 1574-1622.
There are indexed calendars to all the above.

Presentment roll (Grand Jury), 1630-31.

Later judicial records:
Indictment rolls: East Kent, 1639-40, 1650-C20;
West Kent, 1640-C20, (indictments, occasional jury lists, recognizances after 1732).
Recognizance rolls: East Kent, 1649-1730;
West Kent, 1651-1732 (gaps); from 1730-32 incl. in indictment rolls.
Bound volumes of papers, 1640-1714, and composite bundles, 1715-1800 (incl. calendars of prisoners,

County:
Later judicial records, bound volumes, ctd.
jury presentments, depositions, petitions; settlement papers; lists of Papists after 1680; applications for licensing meeting houses after 1689); original sessions bundles, East Kent, 1801-1883, West Kent, 1801-89.

Process books of indictments, 1649-1792 (the volumes form an alphabetical index to all persons indicted, giving names, places of abode and status).

Insolvent debtors, certificates of discharge, lists of creditors, 1691, 1701-1814.

Order books: East Kent, 1653-1931; West Kent 1625-1931.

Minute books, 1677-1835.

Calendars of prisoners, 1627-74, 1702-1706, 1836-1893.

Jurors: original returns, 1696-1824; freeholders books, 1701-1824; Jurors books, 1826-1871.

Licensed tradesmen: victuallers' recognizances, 1574-1621, 1649-1828; lists and registers, 1707-73; alehouse keepers, 1753-1827; badgers, 1753-68 (see *VL*).

Land Tax assessments: 1682-1832; window tax returns, 1705-82, inhabited house tax returns 1777-1786 for Wingham and Maidstone divisons of the county. (see *LWTA*).

Religion, etc.
Register of Declarations against Transubstantiation, 1673-1681.

Sacrament certificates, 1673-1828.

Association rolls, 1696-1702 (subscribed at Maidstone, Canterbury, Ashford, Greenwich and Woolwich, but only c.400 names in all).

Oaths of Allegiance etc., 1702-1874.

Gamekeepers, register of deputations, 1711-1886 (incl. names of manors, lords and gamekeepers, chronologically, indexed from 1783); alphabetical register, 1711-1806 (arranged by name of gamekeeper). Records also under Game Duty taxation, 1784-1807.

Hearth Tax, enrolled assessment, 1664; Marriage Tax, 1705 (see *HT*).

Faversham
Commissions of enquiry, gaol delivery, prosecution of pirates, 1551-1574.
Sessions rolls and papers incl. indictments, frankpledge papers, calendars of prisoners and sessions minutes, 1571-1951; depositions for examinations, 1572-1806; recognizances to appear, 1570-1791.
Oath rolls, declarations and sacrament certificates, 1686-1864.
Recognizances: licensed victuallers, 1570-1836; butchers, meat in Lent, 1586-1622; shipowners, export of grain, 1582-1627.

Kent: *Centre for Kentish Studies, Maidstone* ctd.

Maidstone

(*Note*. Records are derived from several sources, and some catalogue entries appear to overlap.)
Examinations, 1598-1607.
Sessions files, 1642, 1646-1750.
Sessions minutes, 1849-1971.
Writs and jury lists, 1756-1902.
Lists of recognizances, indictments, 1752-59, 1775-1902.
Papers relating to prisoners in gaol, 1649-1853.
Victuallers' recognizances, 1651-85, 1747-61, 1822-28.
Sacrament certificates and oath rolls, 1673-1900.
Certifiicates of dissenters' meeting places, 1831-1851.
Printing press certificates, 1840-45.

Queenborough
Sessions rolls, 1721-1828.
Sessions book, 1819-1885.
Licensed victuallers' recognizances, 1614-1652.
Oaths and sacrament certificates, 1688-1774 (incl. naval officers at Sheerness).

Tenterden
Sessions rolls, 1637-1789.
Nuisance rolls, 1719-1740 (formerly on sessions rolls).
Summary convictions, 1632-1669.
Court books, 1830-1951.
Hearth tax assessment, 1663-1666 (see *HT*).
Victuallers' recognizance rolls and lists, 1676-1706.
Oath rolls, 1661, 1702-1707.

East Kent Archive Centre, Whitefield, Dover.

See also:
<www.kent.gov.uk/e&l/artslib/archives/archek.ac.html>

Deal
(see also under Sandwich, right)
Sessions books, 1719-1899.
Sessions papers and depositions, 1745-1940.
Oath rolls, 1714-1924.
Jury and burgess lists, 1836-1895.

Dover
Minutes, 1836-1952.
Sessions files, 1879-1972.
Calendars of prisoners, 1831-1971.
Oath rolls, 1761, 1803-1846.

New Romney
Sessions books, 1616-1846.
Sessions files, 1590-1819 (10), 1820-73 (34).
Loose court papers, incl. examinations, informations and depositions, indictments, recognizances etc., returns of popish recusants, 1608-1627.
Gaol receiving book, 1849-1855.
Licensed victuallers' recognizances, 1609, 1690-1791 (see also *VL*).
Oaths and sacrament certificates, 1673-1838

East Kent Archive Centre, Dover *continued*

Liberty of Romney Marsh
Sessions books, 1610-1633, 1734-1882.
Sessions rolls, 1819-1873.
Sessions papers, 1742-1825.
Oath rolls, 1727-1903.
Sacrament certificates, 1712-1823.
Appointments of surveyors and overseers, 1738-1851.
Licensing matters, 1710-1851.
Settlement and bastardy examinations, 1779-1847.

Sandwich
Sessions and recognizance books, 1639-1648.
Sessions files, papers and minutes, 1790-1951.
Transportation papers, 1721-1773.
Jurors' books, 1880-1918.
Licensed victuallers' recognizances, 1635-1807 (incl. Ramsgate, Sarre, Deal, Walmer and (infrequently) Brightlingsea in Essex) (see *VL*).
Oath rolls, 1828-1868.

Canterbury Cathedral Archives.

City of Canterbury
Records date from 1461 to 1972, are stored in boxes, more or less one for each year, and most are still awaiting cataloguing.

A full calendar to QS records 1751-1759 (many items in detail) with index (by Duncan Harrington) has been published by Kent FHS on microfiche [no. 164].

For poll books and electoral registers, see *PB* and *ER*; for records of victuallers, see *VL*.

LANCASHIRE

Lancashire Record Office, Preston.

The Q.S. records for the County are described in the Guide to the *Lancashire Record Office*, R.S. France, 3rd edn., 1985.

Sessions rolls date from 1588, calendared and fully indexed to 1606, the rolls 1588-1606 edited by Professor James Tait for Chetham Society, N.S., vol. **77**, 1917. *Manchester sessions: notes of proceedings before Oswald Mosley (1618-30), Nicholas Mosley (1661-72) and Sir Oswald Mosely (1734-39) and other magistrates*, edited by Ernest Axon for Record Society of Lancashire & Cheshire vol. **42**, 1901.

There are unpublished catalogues of the material in the searchroom, although these generally give the year only of an item, e.g. Land Tax, order book etc. and no further information.

Personal and place indexes to the petitions and recogizances are in preparation. Cataloguing of petitions is complete up to 1908. These indexes are now available on the A2A website.

See:
<www.lancashire.gov.uk/education/record_office/services/archives.asp>; *see also*
<A2Adatabase> *and* <archivecat.lancashire.gov.uk>

County
Sessions rolls, 1588-92, 1601-06, 1608-09, 1615-42, 1646-1729, 1736-41, 1744-49 (discontinued in 1750, and replaced by Order Books) (1588-1606 published).
Order books, 1626-43, 1646-66, 1668-75, 1677-1971.
Petitions, 1648-1908.
Recognizances, 1605-06, 1623-43, 1646-58, 1660-1834.
Calendars of prisoners, 1821-69, 1889-1971; Preston only, 1870-73.
Indictment rolls, 1605-06, 1619, 1626-42, 1646-1869.
Indictment books, 1619-26, 1629-36, 1642, 1646-53, 1660-73, 1679-85, 1700-19, 1743-49, 1760-71.
Estreats of fines, 1626-1760 (some gaps).
Insolvent debtors' papers, 1678-1824 (many gaps).
Riot depositions, 1826-1893.
Game preservation registers, 1711-C20.
Jurors: lists, Amounderness and Blackburn Hundred, 1696; Warrington div. of West Derby Hundred, 1708; almost complete for 1776, 1778, 1781, 1784, 1792-1812, 1814-24, 1825-1832.
Licensed tradesmen: alehouse keepers, returns, hundred by hundred, varying completeness, 1619-1828 (many gaps); badgers, 1621-22, 1635-38 (see also *VL*).
Land Tax assessments, 1781-1831 (1780, Salford Hundred only; 1832, Lonsdale, Blackburn and Salford Hundreds only) (see *LWTA*).
Vagrants registers (mainly to Scotland and Ireland), 1801-02, 1811-14, 1818-35.
Oaths and declarations: Sacrament certificates, 1673-1829; also other C18 oaths (and refusals).
Papists: registers and returns 1717-88 (gaps 1777, 1784-87).

Places of worship: registers of Dissenting Meeting houses, 1689-1852; Roman Catholic chapels, 1791-1851.
Registers of parish constables, 1632-37, 1650-58, 1660-64.
Taxation: Hearth Tax, 1664 (Salford, Huncoat and Manchester; exemptions, Ainsworth, Birtle, Castleton, Middleton, Swinton, Urmston and Worsley) (see *HT*);
Poll Tax, 1678 (Bolton division of the Salford Hundred) (see *HT*);
Game Duty, registers, 1784-1789.

Wigan Record Office, Leigh Town Hall

Wigan
Sessions files, 1733-54, 1789-1971. These include jury lists, indictments, recognizances, calendars of prisoners, warrants etc. as well as alehouse recognizances and bastardy bonds. Calendared to 1832.

Q.S. records relating almost exclusively to matters of crime and law and order (no settlement and removal papers and similar 'administrative' records) exist for:

Bolton M.B. Archives, Bolton Central Library

Bolton. Post-trial calendars of prisoners, 1839-1940 (these include names of people convicted, ages, occupations, details of offences etc.);

and for **Manchester**

Manchester Central Library, Archives Unit

for 1839 and from October 1842 on.

For poll books and electoral registers, see *PB* and *ER*; for records of victuallers, see *VL*.

LEICESTERSHIRE

> **The Record Office for Leicestershire, Leicester and Rutland,** Wigston Magna.

See *Quarter Sessions Records in the Leicestershire Records Office*, Gwenith Jones, Leics. R.O. Collections **2**, 1985, £2.75. The records are filed chronologically and are still being listed.

See: <www.leics.gov.uk/record_office.htm> *or email:* <recordoffice@leics.gov.uk> *or* <record-office-catalogue.leics.gov.uk>

County

Rolls (files), 1714-C20 (no gaps), incl. lists of Grand and Petty Juries: presentments; recognizances, C18 and early C19; removal orders, to mid-C19; calendars of prisoners, from mid-C18.

Minute books, 1696-C20 (no gaps) (very brief entries to 1748, fuller later, especially after 1809) incl. registrations, confirmations, licences and enrolments, particularly Dissenting Meeting Houses;

Order books, 1678-1832, with contemporary indexes including one to missing volume, 1665-78.

Jurors, freeholders books, 1775-1833 (including registers of gamekeepers certificates, 1801-07).

Transportations, orders and bonds, 1720-83 (names of felons and place of transportation given in calendar, less than 100 in all).

Licensing: Alehouse recognizance books, 1753-1827 (see *VL*); badgers and drovers, 1766-1771, plus contemporary index.

Register of Oaths, 1714-16; Test Acts Oaths rolls, 1750-1848 (with some sacrament certificates).

Sacrament certificates, 1761, 1764-66, 1773-1827.

Protestant Dissenters: registration rolls of meeting houses, 1714-44, 1760-1841; applications for registration, 1749-1852 (calendar lists places but not personal names); Oath rolls 1753, 1756-57, 1761-1826; also, return of Dissenters' Licences and Teachers' names, 1760-1820.

Papists: registration of estates, 1717-85 (many gaps); papists' registrations, 1715-53 (calendar gives names, 54 in all).

Gamekeepers' deputations, registers, 1717-C20 (incl. index 1717-1822).

Poll books, 1775, 1818, 1841 (MSS); 1719; 1741 (indexed transcript); 1775; 1830; 1857; 1859; 1865; 1867; Borough elections, 1754, 1768, 1796, 1800, 1826, 1832, 1835, 1852 (see *PB*).

Land Tax assessments, 1773-1832, listed in calendar by place with gaps shown (see *LWTA*).

Militia qualifications 1758-C20; Deputy Lieutenants and Militia Officers, names listed in calendar.

Militia returns, 1769, 1775, 1778, 1780-1786 (see *MLM*).

Borough of Leicester

Q.S. records are listed in *The Records of the Corporation of Leicester*, 1956.

Rolls, 1607, 1609, 1617-18, 1626, 1639, 1669, 1671, 1680-1800 (occasional gaps); 1836-1971 [31D71, uncatalogued] (some C19 gaps).

Borough of Leicester, *continued*

Victuallers' recognizances, 1566-72, 1649-62 (gaps), 1681-85, 1710-13, 1716-47.

Assessments of Births, Marriages and Deaths (see *HT*):
St. Mary's parish 1697-1699 [BR.IV.2.7];
St. Martin's 1695/6 [BR.IV.2.7];
St. Margaret's 1699 [BR.IV.2.8].

For electoral registers, see *ER*; for records of victuallers, see *VL*.

LINCOLNSHIRE

> **Lincolnshire Archives,** Lincoln.

For administrative purposes Lincolnshire was divided into the three parts of **Holland**, **Kesteven** and **Lindsey**. Q.S. records for all three are held at the Archives Office, together with those for the City of **Lincoln** and the Boroughs of **Louth**, **Grantham** and **Stamford**. For **Boston** and **Great Grimsby** they are still held locally.

In general there are only summary lists to the records, but there are calendars to Lindsey sessions files, 1625, 1629, 1630 (Ms); Kesteven sessions files, 1628, 1683 (Ts); 1830, Epiphany (Ms); Holland sessions files, 1683, 1684 (Ts). There are no indexes.

There are also Ms calendars of the Hearth Tax returns for Kesteven for 1665-6 and 1670-71 (from Exchequer copy in P.R.O.) with Ms index of names.

See: <www.lincolnshire.gov.uk/archives> *or email:* <lincolnshire.archive@lincolnshire.gov.uk>

The Lincolnshire FHS has produced indexes to the poor law documents within the Q.S. files. Details on their website: <www.genuki.org.uk/big/eng/LIN/lfhs>

Lindsey

Minutes, 1665-78, 1704-12, 1729-1940.
Files, 1625-59, 1702-03, 1730-1971.
Alehouses: register of recognizances, 1632-38; recognizances, 1792-1828 (see *VL*).
Freeholders (jurors) lists: 1717-1922 (not a complete series).
Oaths and declarations: Justices (and Supremacy), various, 1734-1865; Allegiance, 1703-44; Papists, 1717-1809; Dissenters, 1782-1811.

Kesteven

Published: *Minutes of Proceedings in Q.S. held for the parts of Kesteven in the county of Lincoln, 1674-1695*, vols. 1 and 2, ed. S.A. Peyton, in Lincoln Record Society, **25** and **26**, 1931, indexed by persons, place and subjects.

Kesteven QS Settlement Examinations 1700-1847, Lincs FHS. 5 microfiche, 1993

Minutes, 1674-1704 (published to 1695); 1724-1971.
Files, 1682-83, 1686-88, 1694-1707, 1710-89, 1791-1936.
Alehouses: registers of licences, 1678-1729 (missing 1679-83, 1685, 1690, 1711, 1715, 1719, 1723-25, 1727-28); 1732-37; 1755-56; 1784-1812; 1825-65 (see *VL*).

Jurors: Freeholders lists for 1720, 1730-35, 1738, 1740, 1742, 1751-52, 1826-66.

Oaths: register of oaths of Allegiance and Against Transubstantiation, 1689-1857; Papists, 1778-91; protestant dissenters, 1761-1817.

Papists' estates: register roll, 1717.

Holland

Minutes, 1673-84 (rough minutes), 1684-1953.

Files, 1621-22, 1683-85, 1687-1713, 1716-25, 1727-39, 1741-43, 1745-70, 1787-1971.

Alehouses: register of recognizances, 1725-27, 1755-64, 1785, 1787-88 (see *VL*).

Papists' estates register, 1717-1768.

City of Lincoln

Minutes, 1656-63, 1668, 1677-85; 1758-85, 1802-17, 1828-42, 1857-1954.

Minutes of Statute Sessions, 1737-1836.

Hearth Tax, 1662 (see *HT*).

Miscellaneous papers and files 1841-1971.

Borough of Louth

Minutes, 1721-1742.

Borough of Stamford

Minutes, *c.*1624-1630, 1885-1951.

Files, 1629-30, 1633, 1657, 1666, 1710, 1713-37 (broken), 1724, 1732, 1740, 1748, 1750-99, 1801-57 (many in poor condition unfit for consultation).

Minutes, 1730-53, 1818-1824 (at Stamford Town Hall).

Borough of Grantham

Files, 1608, 1610, 1612-19, 1626-27, 1630, 1633, 1635-38.

A detailed catalogue of files between 1608-38 now exists.

Borough of Boston

Minutes, 1729-56, 1780-1827.

Return of prisoners, 1827-34.

Files, 1807-30 (files of depositions, c1858-1904).

Sacrament certificates, 1783-1803.

Oaths of Allegiance, 1782-30.

Alehouse licences: in minutes, 1732-54, 1780-94; in files, 1784-1855, 1870-77 (see *VL*).

North East Lincolnshire Archives, *Grimsby.*

Borough of Great Grimsby

Gaol delivery commissions, 1592-98.

Sessions papers, 1640-1714.

Oaths of Allegiance roll, 1746-52.

Sacrament certificates, 1679-1791.

Declarations against Transubstantiation, 1684 (1 item).

Nothing else survives before 1891.

For Land Tax assessments, poll books and electoral registers see *LWTA, PB* and *ER*; for records of victuallers, see *VL*.

LONDON

City of London Records Office.

The records of this Office are temporarily held at **London Metropolitan Archives** (see page 23). It is intended that official City of London archives will return to Guildhall once the refubishment programme is complete (2008/9).

See: <www.cityoflondon.gov.uk/lma>

Under various royal charters the lord mayor, recorder and aldermen of the City of London were:

(a) Justices of the peace for the City of London. The sessions of the peace, of which there were normally nine or later eight in the year, were opened at Guildhall but adjourned to the Old Bailey. From 1852 only the four Quarter Sessions were held.

(b) Justices of gaol delivery and oyer and terminer for the City of London. The sessions of gaol delivery of which there were normally eight in the year were held at the Old Bailey (Newgate was the gaol for both City and Middlesex prisoners; the records relating to Middlesex cases which were kept separately are now at the London Metropolitan Archives).

In some respects these sessions records are comparable to assize records for a county.

(c) Justices of the peace for the borough of Southwark -- see under Surrey (page 31).

Prior to 1785 the records under (a) and (b) were kept in the same series of books, files etc. From 1785 there are separate series of books, files etc., for peace and gaol delivery. The lord mayor and aldermen's jurisdiction as justices of gaol delivery came to an end in 1834 upon the establishment of the Central Criminal Court.

The official archives of Peace, Gaol Delivery and Oyer and Terminer, comprise:

Files (one per session, containing when complete the calendar, indictments, recognizances, jury lists): July 1568; July 1603; 1605-22, 1639, 1649, 1651-1661 (certain files missing for most of these years); 1662-1785.

Minute books: 1612-13, 1662-1785.

Papers (depositions, affidavits, petitions etc.): 1648-1785 (very incomplete especially in the earlier years).

As mentioned, after 1785 records of Peace, and of Gaol Delivery and Oyer and Terminer, were separated. For the former they run continuously from 1785 to C20. For the latter Files and Minute Books are complete, 1785-1834, but other papers are missing or incomplete for most years.

Note. Except during the Commonwealth period records are in Latin until 1732. The clerk's annotations as to sentencing etc. are often highly abbreviated. In addition, the Sessions records include a variety of returns, registers and papers of the Clerk of the Peace.

London (C.L.R.O./L.M.A.) continued

Returns in the Sessions records include, *inter alia:*
Registers of Hair Powder Duty Certificates, 1795-98.
Lists of insolvent debtors, 1719-1816.
Schedules of estates of insolvent debtors, 1671-1820.
Papists, miscellaneous lists and returns, 1673-1747.
Warrants for the removal of Scottish and Irish paupers, 1834-1846.
Hearth Tax, 1670-73; Subsidies, Aids etc., 1661-97; Marriage Tax, 1695 (index published in *London Inhabitants within the Walls, 1695*, introduction by D.V. Glass, London R.S., **2**, 1966) (see *HT*).

Indexes: Personal name indexes to persons indicated (Ms), 1714-1834 (4 vols.); Sessions of Peace only, 1835, 1855-1927.
Personal name card index of insolvent debtors' schedules, 1755-1820.
The general subject card index gives particulars of certain classes of Sessions records.
Ts list of dates of Sessions indicating whether books, files or calendars survive.
Ms list of Sessions papers indicating dates for which papers survive (only to Jan. 1785).

Additionally, reference to reports of some trials can be obtained from the following publications:
The Complete Book of Emigrants, 1661-1699, by P.W. Coldham, 1990.
Bonded Passengers to America, by P.W. Coldham, 1983, of which vol. **2** covers Middlesex cases, 1677-1775, and vol. **3** London cases, 1656-1775. This supersedes the same author's *English Convicts in Colonial America*, 1974-6. Both give a year and month or quarter of sentence, from which a report could probably be traced, although actual references to Sessions papers are not given.
Lists of Indentured servants, based on records of judicial origin in the Records Office, are published in *A list of Emigrants from England to America, 1682-1692*, by M. Ghirelli, 1968; *A list of Emigrants ... 1718-1759*, by J. and M. Kaminkow, 1964 (both Magna Charta Book Co.), and *Emigrants to America: Indentured Servants Recruited in London 1718-1733*, by John Wareing, 1985 (Genealogical Publishing Co., Baltimore). Some of these may in the process of revision by P.W. Coldham.
Reports of trials at the Old Bailey were published in *The Proceedings on the King's Commissions of the peace, oyer and terminer and gaol delivery*, usually known as *Old Bailey sessions papers*. Despite the title these do not include reports of Sessions of the Peace but they do cover Gaol Delivery and Oyer and Terminer for both the City of London and for Middlesex to 1834, and thereafter Central Criminal Court cases to 1913. The published reports are often the best source of information as to evidence given by witnesses etc.
The Records Office has a few of these published reports for 1683-85 and others 1777-1913 (with gaps), but there is a better run at Guildhall Library.

Guildhall Library, London.

See *A guide to genealogical sources in Guildhall Library*, R. Harvey, 4th ed., 1997; and 'Familia': <www.org.uk/services/london/corp_of_london.html>

The dates of the catalogued sequence of *Sessions Papers* held in the Library are as follows:

Dec. 1684 - Feb. 1688 (incomplete); April 1707 - May 1728 (incomplete); Dec. 1729 - Oct. 1741 (complete); April 1742 - Oct. 1743 (incomplete); Dec. 1744 - April 1913 (complete).

There are also occasional separately catalogued reports of individual sessions, the earliest dating from 1673.

Contents: The *Sessions Papers* consist of reports of cases held at the Sessions House in the Old Bailey (from 1834, in the Central Criminal Court), giving names of defendants, verdicts and sentences, and purportedly verbatim transcripts of the evidence. No personal details are given of defendants, apart from their ages, and anything which can be gleaned from the evidence. In addition to names of defendants and witnesses, names of justices and at various periods jurors and counsel are given.
There are isolated reports of cases held in other courts, such as Assizes for Surrey, Essex, Kent and Hertfordshire (for example, in 1773-5).

Indexes: Indexes to names of defendants are available from the mayoral year 1731-2 onwards. Originally they cover the whole mayoral year, later, just individual monthly sessions. The Library also holds a collection (not necessarily complete) of indexes compiled by Barnett and Buckler, shorthand writers, to mayoral years from 1835 to 1893-4.
Additionally, references to reports of some trials can be obtained from the following published sources:
The Crimes of the First Fleet Convicts, comp. John Cobley, 1970, giving details of those transported to Australia in the 'First Fleet' of 1787, incl. references to the 'Sessions Papers' for those tried at the Old Bailey; and *The Founders of Australia: A Biographical Dictionary of the First Fleet*, by Mollie Gillen, 1989 (Sydney).

For the magnificent series of Land Tax assessments, 1692-94, 1703-1949 held by Guildhall Library, see *LWTA*.

For poll books and electoral registers, see *PB* and *ER*; for records of victuallers, see *VL*.

For County of London Sessions of the Peace records, 1889-1971, see under 'Middlesex'.

MIDDLESEX and WESTMINSTER

Published: *Middlesex County Records, 1549-1688*, vols. 1-4, J.C. Jeafferson, 1886-92 (Middlesex County Record Soc.); *Calendar of Sessions Books, 1689-1709*, 1 vol., 1905, N.N., *1612-1618*, 4 vols., 1935-41 (Middlesex C.C.).

London Metropolitan Archives *(formerly G.L.R.O.).*

The sessions records deriving from four commissions, the Commissions of the Peace for the County of Middlesex, the Commission of Oyer and Terminer, the Commission of the Peace for the City and Liberty of Westminster, and the Commission of Gaol Delivery of Newgate, have been described as a 'body of muniments which, relating as they do to the history of the metropolitan county from Elizabeth to Victoria, may safely be said to surpass in interest, as they probably do in extent, the records of any other county in England'.

Fortunately for those considering using these records, they have been admirably described in the *Guide to the Middlesex Sessions Records* (Greater London C.C., 1965), which is essential introductory reading, as, in the view of the head archivist, 'they are not a series to be tackled without careful preparation'.

Amongst classes of records which readers may decide are of particular interest to them (*after* reading the *Guide*) are the following:

See also: <www.cityoflondon.gov.uk/Corporation/ leisure_heritage/libraries_archives_museums_ galleries/lma/htm/records_held_htm>

Middlesex Sessions

Justices of the Peace
Commissions of the Peace, 1689-1878.
Commissions of Oyer and Terminer, 1689-1831.
Qualification oaths, 1745-1889.
Oaths of office, 1761-1867.
Lists of justices, 1710-1971.

The Court in session
Sessions of the Peace and Oyer and Terminer rolls, 1549-1971.
Sessions of the Peace registers, 1608-1667.
Sessions of the Peace and Oyer and Terminer books, 1639-1889.
Process registers of indictments, 1610-1775.
Instruction books of indictments, 1728-1756.
'Book of Informations', 1624-1639.
Calendars of indictments etc., 1684-1797, 1833-1971.
Calendars of prisoners, 1559-1971.
Sessions papers, 1689-C19.
Insolvent debtors' petitions, 1671-1812.

Enrolment, registration and deposit
Plantation indentures (America and West Indies) 1683-84 (see *A List of Emigrants*, page 22).
Jurors: lists of freeholders 1696-1889.
Licensing: victuallers, 1552, 1716-1829 (see *VL*); gamekeepers 1728-1867; butchers 1632.
Religion: sacrament certificates, 1673-1825; Oath rolls, 1673-1873; Recusants, 1675-1764.

Middlesex Sessions: *Enrolment etc. continued*

Taxation: Hearth Tax, 1664, 1669-1674 (see *HT*).Parliamentary elections:
Annuities, 1779-1846;
Land Tax assessments, 1767, 1780-1832 (see *LWTA*);
Poll Books, 1749, 1768-69, 1806 (see *PB*).

Westminster Sessions

Justices of the Peace
Commissions of the Peace, 1687-1837.
Lists of justices 1689-1756, 1785.
Returns, 1835.

The Court in session
Sessions of the Peace rolls, 1620-1844.
Sessions books, 1641-1844.
Process register of indictments, 1660-79.
Sessions papers, 1689-1844.

Enrolment, registration and deposit
Jurors: freeholders' books, 1728, 1792.
Victuallers' licences, 1690-1793 (see *VL*).
Land Tax assessments, 1767, 1781, 1797-1832 (see *LWTA*).
Poll books, 1749-1820 (see *PB*).
Sacrament certificates, 1673-1825.
Oath rolls, 1673-1837.
Recusants, 1657-1722.
Hearth Tax, 1664, 1672-1674 (see *HT*).

Gaol Delivery Sessions
Rolls, 1549-1836;
Registers, 1608-1679.
Books, 1639-1834.
Papers, 1674-1792.
Calendars of indictments, 1754-1832.
Newgate calendars, 1820-22, 1830-1853.

The foregoing is an arbitrary selection from the contents list of the aforementioned Guide, intended merely to give an indication of period of survival for just a few of the classes of records in this vast archive.

County of London Sessions

This court came into operation on 1 April 1889. Its jurisdiction was the newly created administrative county of London. It ceased to operate in December 1971.

The Court in Session
Sessions of the Peace rolls, 1889-1971.
Calendars of prisoners, 1889-1965.

Bedfordshire & Luton Archives & Records Service, *Bedford.*

Calendars of prisoners at Q.S. include Middlesex prisoners, 1863-1879.

For electoral registers, see *ER*; for records of victuallers, see *VL*.

MONMOUTHSHIRE – see with **Wales**, page 39.

NORFOLK

Norfolk Record Office, Norwich.

The Record Office has Q.S. records for the **County** and for **Norwich** and **Great Yarmouth**. See also boroughs of **King's Lynn** and **Thetford**.
A Calendar of the *Norfolk Q.S. Order Book , 1650-1657*, by D.E. Howell James, is published as Norfolk Record Society, **26**, 1955.

See also <norfrec@norfolk.gov.uk>

County

Sessions books, 1565-68, 1572-77, 1582-86, 1629-1644, 1649-54, 1661-76, 1684-93, 1710-18, 1727-1749, 1752-1955.
Order books, 1650-81, 1689-1721, 1724-35, 1749-1773, 1784-1791.
Files, 1532-1807 (with gaps).
Minute books, 1799-1968.
Visiting Justices of the Gaol Committee minute book, 1809-1814. (Minute books, 1820-56, 1864-72 and report books, 1844-77, are in Norwich Castle Museum.)
Wymondham Magistrates' Bridewell Committee minute book, 1832-1864.
Registers of convictions: general, 1855-1955; juvenile, 1847-1881; night poaching, 1829-1954.
Calendars of prisoners, 1862-1971 (also assize prisoners, 1863-1922. 1952-1971).
Recognizance books, 1847-1870.
Indictments and recognizances, 1890-1927.
Estreat rolls, 1822-1946.
Insolvent debtors' petitions (57), 1725.
Appeals against removal orders, 1720-1728.
Returns of pauper lunatics, 1900-1924.
Reports of Visitors to Loddon Lunatic Asylum, 1827-1845.
Deeds of bargain and sale, 1560/1-1731/2 (cal. by J.C. Tingey in *Norfolk Archaeology* **13**).
Declarations against Transubstantiation, 1673-1700; oaths of allegiance etc., 1689-1849 (with gaps); Dissenting preachers' oaths, 1796-1824; oaths and declarations of Roman Catholics, 1791-1834.
Sacrament certificates, 1689-1808 (with gaps). With Ts personal names index.
Papists' estates: registers, 1717-77 (indexed); returns, 1717, 1759-1779 (with Ts list of personal names).
Grants of annuity: registers, 1756-1807, 1818-1848 (with index of grantors and annuitants); certificates, 1763-1842 (with Ts calendar).
Freemasons: lists of members, 1867-1968 (gaps).
Land Tax Assessments, 1767-1832 (see *LWTA*).
Gamekeepers: registers of deputations to, 1784-92, 1851-92 (with index of gamekeepers and lords of manor).
Licensed victuallers and alehouse keepers: lists of recognizances, 1634, 1648-1673, 1808; register, 1789-1799 (with index by parish) (see *VL*).
Officers' appointments and oaths: sheriffs, and undersheriffs, 1820-1933 (with Ts lists of names).

Justices: commissions of peace, 1689-1878; oaths, 1761-63, 1830-1914.

City of Norwich

Sessions books or minute books, 1511-50, 1553-56, 1561-1618, 1629-1971.
Search books (alphabetical lists of persons indicted at City and County Sessions), 1623-80 (City) and 1624-74 (County).
Files: indictments and recognizances, 1538, 1547, 1554, 1563-1749 (a few gaps), 1760-1838.
Files: interrogations and depositions, 1549-54, 1557-1600, 1648, 1684-1711, 1717, 1722-65, 1770-90.
Files, 1921-71.
Grand Jury presentments, 1692-1835.
Returns of prisoners, 1681-82, 1702-1833.
List of prisoners (indexed), 1836-1903.
Cases books, 1867-1971.
Registers of convictions, 1836-1944.
Copies of depositions of witnesses, 1855-90.
Recorders' notebooks, 1859-60, 1960-71.
Minute books of administrative business, 1839-1955.
Visiting Justices to Norwich Gaol: order books, 1846-1878.
Visiting Justices to Norwich Infirmary Asylum: minutes, 1845-60, 1862-64.
Rating: appeals to poor rates, 1724-1859.
Debtors: schedules (listing debtor's estate and effects and his creditors) and discharges of, 1678-1781 (with gaps).
Registers of settlement examinations, 1754-1811.
Removal orders, 1686-1829.
Orders for passing vagrants, with examinations, 1740, 1747-64.
Constables' charges for conveyance of (named) soldiers, sailors and families, 1756-61.
Bastardy orders, depositions etc. (15), 1689-1711, 1733, 1734, 1808.
Clerk of Peace's correspondence, 1921-71.
Estreats of fines, 1845-1971.
Signatories to Solemn League and Covenant, 1644, and signatories against, 1677-1719; declarations against Transubstantiation, 1673-81, 1684-88; of Anglican clergy, 1767-1844, of Roman Catholics, 1778 and 1791, and of schoolmasters, 1812-23; subscribers to fund for repression of rebellion, 1745.
Sacrament certificates, 1713-1827. With Ts personal names index.
Papists' estates: returns, 1717, 1723, 1745.
Land Tax assessments, 1710-1832 (almost complete), together with window tax, 1708, 1710-1760s (with gaps) (see *LWTA*).
Licensed victuallers and alehouse keepers: register, 1596-1604; original recognizances, 1760-1807 (with Ts index of alehouses and licencees). (Pre-1760 entered in sessions minute books.) (see *VL*)
Officers' appointments and oaths; surveyors of highways, 1767-1837.

Norfolk: *N.R.O., Norwich,* continued

Great Yarmouth
Summary list published in the *Guide to the Great Yarmouth Borough Records*, Paul Rutledge, 1972.

Sessions records attached to court rolls, 1502-03, 1509-21, 1523-24, 1531-1623, 1630-51, 1661-1676.
Sessions books, 1567-94, 1597-1702, 1704-1732.
Waste (draft) sessions books, 1640-44, 1676-88, 1707-96, 1811-1864.
Sessions files, 1700-1863, 1945-71. Highway sessions file, 1743-98.
Justices' order books, 1715-1836. (Visiting Justices of the Gaol order book, 1846-75 and minutes 1843-76 are held by the Great Yarmouth Museums).
Test rolls, 1673-1853.
Recorder's minutes, 1872-80, 1882-83, 1887-93, 1914-68.
Register of appeals, 1898-1958.
Clerk's case books, 1911-64.

King's Lynn
(held by **Borough Council of King's Lynn & West Norfolk** at *Town Hall, King's Lynn*; access can be arranged by appointment through the Norfolk R.O.).

Sessions books, 1726-1858, 1866-1957.
Minute books, 1620-1685, 1729-1865.
Oath rolls, 1689-95, 1718-1847.
Miscellaneous papers, C18-C19.

Thetford
(held by **Thetford Town Council**, at *King's House, Thetford*; list available in Norfolk R.O.)

Sessions books, 1610-1626, 1632/3-1639.
Minute books, 1751-1833, 1839-1951.
Files, 1897-98, 1938-51.
Jury lists, 1894-1914.
Recorder's notebooks, 1937-1947.
Licensing sessions minutes, 1682-86 (see *VL*).
Clerk of the Peace's letter book, 1916-23.
Licensed victuallers and alehouse keepers: recognizances, 1571-1584 (with gaps), 1620-29 (see *VL*).
Apprentices: enrolments, 1528, 1531.
Officers' appointments: visitors and clerk under 1860 Lunacy Act, 1894-1903.
Justices: commissions of peace, 1833-72; oaths, 1830-1926.

For poll books and electoral registers, see *PB* and *ER*; for records of victuallers, see *VL*.

NORTHAMPTONSHIRE

Northamptonshire Record Office, *Northampton.*

The Record Office holds Q.S. records for **Northamptonshire**, for the Liberty (or Soke) of **Peterborough**, and also for the Borough of **Northampton**.
The earliest records for the County are published in *Quarter Sessions Records of Northamptonshire, 1630, 1657, 1657/8*, ed. Joan Wake, Northamptonshire Record Society, **1**, 1924, fully indexed.
There are very few finding aids, but there are lists of Northamptonshire records for the periods 1630, 1657-1672, 1800-1968, and a card index to the Record Book, 1738-1754.
Records for Peterborough, 1700-1702, were transcribed by W.T. Mellows, 1938.
Northamptonshire Quarter Sessions: Gamekeepers Index 1711-1932, ed. Kay Collins pub. Northamptonshire FHS. *Northamptonshire Quarter Sessions: Meeting House Index 1699-1707, 1737-1788*, ed. Kay Collins, Northamptonshire FHS.

See also <archivist@northamptonshire.gov.uk>

Northamptonshire
Rolls/Files, 1630, 1657-1972.
Minute books, 1668-1965.
Record/Order books 1685-1707, 1738-1912.
Presentments, 1693-1790.
Recognizances, 1672-1846.
Alehouse keepers' recognizances, 1692, 1737-1828 (see *VL*).
Freeholders' lists, 1699-1926.
Jury Lists (not in book form), 1823-1923.
Taxes (Poll, Marriage, Window etc.), 1691-1702, Rothwell, Corby, Huxloe hundreds (see *HT*).
Land Tax assessments from 1752 (see *LWTA*).

Liberty of Peterborough
Rolls, 1699-1710, 1872-1917, 1923-65.
Record books, 1756-1787, 1795-1965.
Land Tax assessments, listed by parish in *Genealogical Sources in Cambridgeshire* (Cambs. R.O.) (see also *LWTA*).

The foregoing are of indirect use to family historians, but are not easy to use.

Borough of Northampton
Rolls or files, 1745-1902 (including depositions from c.1880).

For poll books and electoral registers, see *PB* and *ER*; for records of victuallers, see *VL*.

NORTHUMBERLAND

Northumberland Record Office,
North Gosforth, Newcastle upon Tyne.

The Record Office issues a leaflet concisely listing the various classes of Northumberland Q.S. records held. There are a subject index and various sectional lists and calendars but no index of personal names.

See also: <www.northumberland.gov.uk>

The Northumberland & Durham FHS has published the following indexes on microfiche; *Newcastle upon Tyne Quarter Sessions Indexes 1744-7, 1818-55 & 1867-76*; *Northumberland & Durham Quarter Sessions and Assize Courts newspaper index 1792-1829 & 1830-1851.*

County
Sessions Order Books, 1680-1889 (1680-86 in Latin, presentments, indictments and recognizances, not typical of series as a whole; remainder are in English). Subject index to 1850, calendared to 1822.
Indictments, 1771-1807, catalogued and indexed.
Indictment book, 1580-1630 (the only early Q.S. record).
Jurors' lists, 1763-1824; jury books, 1826-78; jury list returns, 1749- 1813 (many gaps).
Registers of alehouse keepers' recognizances, 1822-1828 (see *VL*).
Militia officers, certificates etc., 1757-1883.
Land Tax returns, 1748-1831 (see *LWTA*).
County (Navy Quota Act) returns of men, carts and carriages, 1795-96 (see *MLM*).
Religious returns: Roman Catholic estates, 1717-1789 (published in Surtees Society, **131**, 1918).

Berwick upon Tweed Record Office.

See: <www.bpears.org.uk/NRO/Berwick.html>

Berwick upon Tweed County Borough
Q.S. books, 1694-1781, 1812-29, 1879-1951).
Indictments, 1698-1855.
Informations, 1698-1855.
Examinations, 1700-1810, 1836-67.
Recognizances, 1702-1855.
Jury lists, 1715-1818, 1836-67.
Alehouse recognizances, 1767-1779, 1810-1822 (see *VL*).
Coroners' inquisitions, 1745-1851 (indexed).
Lists of freemasons, 1799-1814.
Sacrament certificates, 1688-1827.
QS bundles 1856-1951 - from 1856 all papers relating to each court were kept in bundles. They include convictions, informations, reconizances, coroners' inquisiations etc.

An interim list is available. The records with a few exceptions are not indexed.

Tyne and Wear Archives Service,
Newcastle upon Tyne.

See User Guide **14**, *Court and Police Records* (s.a.e.); and <tyneandweararchives.org.uk>

Newcastle upon Tyne
Order books, 1646-47 (recognizances only), 1650-51, 1665-71, 1700-1802 (incl. recognizances); 1804-12 (draft minutes); 1818-55, 1867-1971. Indexed 1818-55, 1867-76.
Sessions minute books, 1839-1911.
Draft minutes, 1782-96, 1804-12.
Sessions files, 1672-77, 1693, 1694-1716, 1728, 1743-49, 1751-62, 1767-80, 1783-85, 1807, 1828, 1830-34.
Recorder's notebooks, 1889-90, 1899-1901, 1903-1909, 1911-14, 1919-23, 1948-56, 1970-71.
Official notebooks, 1892, 1895-98.
Calendars of prisoners, 1837, 1840-48, 1880-92.
Registers of oaths, 1839-42.
Depositions of witnesses and examinations of prisoners, 1827-29, 1849.
Recognizances to appear as witness, 1828.
Recognizances in filiation cases, 1828.
Conviction certificates, 1828, 1843.
Poor law and settlement papers, 1827-1834.
Bastardy registers, 1844-76, 1893-1961.
Clerk's correspondence, 1837-1922, 1929-32, 1947-1969.
Cash books, 1820-1835.
Register of alehouses, 1822-1828 (see *VL*).
Register of names and property of Papists and others refusing to take the Oath of Allegiance, 1717-1783 etc.

For poll books and electoral registers, see *PB* and *ER*; for records of victuallers, see *VL*.

NOTTINGHAMSHIRE

Nottinghamshire Archives, Nottingham.

The Archives Office holds Q.S. records for the **County** and also for the Boroughs of **Nottingham** and **Newark**. Most are listed briefly in the *Guide to the Nottinghamshire Records Office*, P.A. Kennedy, 1961.

There are Ts lists to all records, some Ts abstracts of C18 Nottinghamshire records. Card indexes, 1723-1858, for Nottingham only, to
(1) Persons transported;
(2) Maintenance orders (bastardy), this index is currently being updated to include orders recorded in the Q.S.;
(3) Removal orders.

See also:
<www.nottinghamshire.gov.uk/home/leisure/archives> *or email:* <archives@nottscc.gov.uk>

Selections only have been published in *Nottinghamshire County Records of the 17th Century*, H.H. Copnall, 1915; *Nottinghamshire County Records of the 18th Century*, K.T. Beaby, 1947; *Records of the Borough of Nottingham*, 9 vols., 1888-1956.

The Nottinghamshire FHS has published several abstracts from the Quarter Sessions. Details can be found on their website: <www.nottsfhs.org.uk>

Nottinghamshire: *Notts Archives, Nottingham ctd.*

County

Minute books, 1603-42, 1652-1971; indictments only, 1676-1704; recognizances only, 1667-1695.
Rolls/files, 1675-1971.
Jury lists and Grand Jury lists, 1760-1804.
Lists of Freeholders qualified to serve on jury, 1732, 1739, 1780-81, 1786-1824.
Oaths: Allegiance etc., 1714-1858;
Sacrament certificates, rolls and registers, 1689-1727;
Dissenting ministers, Quakers and Papists, 1737-1811.
Calendars of prisoners, County Gaol, 1722-1971 (with gaps); Southwell, 1823-37, 1850-53; Wakefield, 1831.
Lists of debtors in County Gaol, 1725-1813; Basford, 1725-1811.
Game: certificate lists, 1784-97, 1858; registers of deputations for gamekeepers, 1711-1958.
Licences: printing presses, 1819-60; slaughter houses, 1786-99; alehouse recognizances, 1809-1827 (see *VL*).
Religion: registers of papists' estates, 1717-20 (with index); enrolments, 1723-1779.
Land Tax assessments, 1780-1832, and some earlier (see *LWTA*).

Nottingham

Rolls, 1452-1971 (with gaps).
Minutes and draft minutes, 1723-1971 (with gaps).

Newark

Rolls, 1773-99, 1927-71.
Minutes, 1720-1908, 1951-68.

For poll books and electoral registers, see *PB* and *ER*; for records of victuallers, see *VL*.

OXFORDSHIRE

Oxfordshire Record Office, Cowley, Oxford.

Oxfordshire RO holds Q.S. records for the **County** and for **Banbury**, **Chipping Norton** and **Henley** boroughs. **Oxford City** Q.S. records are also available there.

See also: <www.oxfordshire.gov.uk/oro> and email: <archives@oxfordshire.gov.uk>

County

The County records start in 1687 and are described by H.M. Walton in 'Q.S. Records in Oxfordshire and their Use for the Genealogist', *Oxon. Family Histn.*, **2**, 4 (Spring 1981) and, more briefly, by Shirley Barnes in 'Genealogical Sources in the Oxfordshire County Record Office', *Oxon. FH*, **1**, 5 (Summer 1978).

A full calendar of the earliest rolls, 1687-1689, is published in *Oxfordshire Justices of the Peace in C17* (134-page Appendix), Mary Sturge Gretton, Oxon. Record Society, **16**, 1934.

Oxfordshire: *Oxfordshire.R.O. continued*

There is a full Ms calendar, with personal and subject index, to the Q.S. rolls from 1687 to 1830, compiled by Canon W.J. Oldfield. This includes: Depositions, recognizances, indictments, orders of removal, jury lists, calendar of prisoners, gamekeepers' deputations, recusants.

Oxfordshire Family History Society have recently published a DVD covering the whole of this magnificent calendar (<www.ofhs.org.uk>). Copies at Oxfordshire Studies (Oxford Central Library) and Holford Centre (OFHS). The Oxfordshire Q.S. records are therefore amongst the easiest there are to use. There is also a place name index to much of the calendar at Oxfordshire Record Office.
Calendars of Prisoners tried at Oxford Q.S. and Assize Courts, 1831-35, 1836-39, 1840-42 (3 parts), pub. Oxfordshire Blacksheep Publications, stocked by OFHS (as above).

Other Q.S. records (not calendared); Q.S. Rolls, 1830-1966 are uncatalogued.
Minute books, 1689-1944.
Record (minute) books, 1761-1965 (with contemporary indexes);
Register of gamekeepers' deputations, 1784-1925 (indexed);
Register of victuallers' recognizances, 1752-1822 (see *VL*); published for 1769 (and for Oxford, Chipping Norton, Woodstock), by The EurekA Partnership (see under Bucks, page 6; and stocked by OFHS, as above).
Register of Papists' estates, 1715;
Land Tax assessments, 1785-1832 (also 1760 for Ploughley and Wootton Hundreds) (see *LWTA*).
Additonal classes exist – see the A2A website for details.

Oxford City

Minutes 1687-1832 (gaps 1712, 1776-90).
Proceedings, 1823-1835.
Rolls, 1737-C20.
Order Books, 1614-38, 1657-76, 1678-1719, 1746-1747, 1820-1880.
Note. A calendar of the Order Book, 1614-37, awaits publication by Oxford Historical Society.

Banbury Borough

Minute book, 1876-1945; Costs book, 1864-1945.
No other Q.S. records survive.

Henley Borough

Minutes, 1723-1871.
Oaths of Allegiance, 1742-46, 1770; roll, 1779-1823.
List of jurors, 1810.
Sacrament certificates, 1736-54 (94), 1774-76 (10).

Chipping Norton Borough

Oaths, sacrament certificates, jury lists etc., 1780-1835. Now catalogued – see the A2A website for details.

For poll books and electoral registers, see *PB* and *ER*; for records of victuallers, see *VL*.

RUTLAND

The Record Office for Leicestershire, Leicester and Rutland, *Wigston Magna.*

The Record Office holds the few surviving Q.S. records (no Sessions Rolls) for Rutland, most having been destroyed ('sent for salvage') in 1939.
See *Quarter Sessions Records in the Leicestershire Record Office*, Gwenith Jones, Leics. R.O. Collections **2**, 1985, £2.75.

See also: <recordoffice@leics.gov.uk>
or <record-office.catalogue.leics.gov.uk>

County
Minute books, 1742-1774, 1772-1802, including presentments, pleas, verdicts, sentences, recognizances, orders, gamekeepers' deputations.
Minute book series, 1802-09, 1815-1914, contemporary indexes 1802-09, 1815-39.

For Land Tax assessments, poll books and electoral registers, see *LWTA*, *PB* and *ER*.

SHROPSHIRE

Shropshire Archives, *Shrewsbury.*

The Archive holds the Q.S. records for the **County** and for the boroughs of **Shrewsbury, Ludlow Bridgnorth** and **Much Wenlock.**

See <www.shropshire.gov.uk/archives>
or email: <archives@shropshire-cc.gov.uk>

The Q.S. order books were published in *County of Salop: Abstracts of Q.S. Orders, 1638-1889*, 4 vols., Salop. C.C., 1899-1915, with subject, person and place index. Abstracts of Q.S. Rolls, 1820-30, for the County of Salop, with subject and place index, was published by the County Records Committee, 1974.
Shropshire FHS has published a CD (2006) - Quarter Sessions Index 1830-1920.
<www.sfhs_org_uk/Documents/SFHS_Publication.pdf>

County
Order (and draft order) books, 1638-1874 (full calendar published).
Minutes, 1708-1800, 1840-C20.
Rolls, from 1696, incomplete until after 1761. A full list with partial abstract of contents was published by Salop C.C., c.1902, unindexed. Includes indictments, recognizances, depositions; jury lists; lists of coroners, bailiffs, constables, and licensed victuallers; names of prisoners; bastardy and settlement orders; sacrament certificates.
Files, 1731-1888.
Newspaper reports of Q.S. business, 1857-1889.
Process and indictment books, 1722-1841.
Calendars of prisoners, 1786-1845, 1858-1930.

Shropshire: County *continued*
General recognizances, registers, 1700-1789, 1823-1832.
Insolvent debtors, entry book, 1730-85.
Oaths and certificates: sacrament, 1699-1700, 1704, 1718-26; others, 1738-1808.
Alehouse keepers, recognizances, registers, 1753-1828 (see *VL*).
Badgers, 1631, 1651-1660, 1714.
Gamekeepers' registers, 1711-1807.
Electors: Land Tax, 1799 (Franchise of Wenlock, only survival) (see *LWTA*).
Polling lists, 1713, 1714, 1832 (see *PB*).
Registers of electors, 1833-34, 1836, 1864, 1873 and later (see *ER*).
Jurors, freeholders book, 1808 only.
Register of papists' estates, 1717-90.

Bridgnorth
Order books, 1696-1836; files 1634-1858.
Alehouse/victuallers' recognizances, Alehouse licensing records including recognizances 1675-1828 (see *VL*).

Shrewsbury
See *Calendar of Shrewsbury Borough Records, 1896*, incl. Q.S. records, late C17-C18.

Rolls, writs, files, arranged by year.
Minutes and order books, lists of names.

Ludlow
Minute book, 1752-1848.
Order book with victuallers' recognizances, 1706-1741 (see *VL*).
Recognizance books, incl. alehouse keepers, 1577-1810 (see *VL*).
Licensed victuallers, 1742-1798 (see *VL*).
Sacrament certificates, 1691-1818.

Wenlock
Order books, 1788-1836.
Examinations, 1729-53, 1774-77, 1796-1801, 1830-1840.
Removal orders, 1718-1844.
Bastardy examinations, 1799-1802, 1811-36.
Pauper apprenticeship indentures, 1800-1831.
Bonds, 1659-1797.
Alehouse keepers, recognizances, registers, 1764-1851.
Coroners' inquisitions, 1616, 1664-67, 1702-03, 1725-26, 1735, 1745, 1751-59, 1804-36, 1917-27.
Files, 1598-99, few C17 and C18, 1810-36, 1842-45, 1884-1914, 1920-46, 1947-51.

For late C17 taxes, Land Tax assessments, poll books and electoral registers, see *HT*, *LWTA*, *PB* and *ER*; for records of victuallers, see *VL*.

Oswestry Town Council *(c/o Town Clerk)*

Oswestry
Order books, 1737-1836.

SOMERSET

Somerset Archive and Record Service, Taunton.

The Q.S. records for the county are described in an *Interim Handlist of Q.S. documents* (1947) and an extended version of this remains the most detailed finding list, although more precise catalogues of certain sections of the records have since been prepared (e.g., gaol records and county bridge papers).

There is a card index of persons, places and subjects in the Sessions Rolls, 1607-1616, 1660-1730.

Order books, 1607-1676, published by Somerset Record Society, **23**, **24**, **28**, **34**; enrolled deeds of Bargain and Sale, 1537-1656 (S.R.S., *51*).

Sessions rolls are now fully calendared on the Archive and Record Service website <www.somerset.gov.uk/archives> for 1561, 1591, 1597, 1607-16, 1665-69, 1685-90, 1700-50.

See also Email: <archives@somerset.gov.uk>

County
Order books, 1613-1971 (gaps 1638-46, 1656-65, 1774-84).
Sessions rolls, 1561, 1591, 1597, 1607-1639, 1642, 1644-45, 1647-66, 1668-1721, 1725-1970.
Recognizance books, 1597-1848.
Recognizance rolls, 1607-1895.
Indictment rolls, 1571-1889.
Process books of indictments, 1607-1850.
Estreat books of fines, 1586-1905.
Oath rolls, sacrament certificates etc., 1673-1859.
Papists' estate rolls and files, 1717-1788.
Freeholders' books, 1714.
Land Tax assessments, 1766-67, 1780-1832 (see *LWTA*).
Electoral registers, 1832 to date (see *ER*).
Poll books, 1807-1837 (see *PB*).
Gamekeepers' deputations and registers, 1726-1940.
Victuallers' and alehouse keepers' recognizances, 1608-1830 (see *VL*).
List of Chelsea Pensioners in Somerset, 1836 (150) [Q/C 11/6].
Warrants conveying convicts to gaol (arranged by district) [Q/FA 22, 23], Summons sheets (by district) [Q/AP 89/13], both 1749-on.
List of parish constables (by district) [Q/AP 84-86], 1842-73.
Police charge sheets [Q/AP 19-29], 1856-on.
Jury lists and books, 1608-1865 (*Somerset Jurors List 1748*, comp. A.J. Webb, Harry Galloway Publishing, 2nd edn. 1993 (£10 incl. p&p), 39 Nutwell Rd, Worle, Weston-s-Mare BS22 0EW).

Bridgwater
Limited C18 volumes and papers evidently covering both Petty and Quarter Sessions. Otherwise no pre-C20 records.

Bath & North East Somerset Record Office.

See *Avon Local History Handbook*, ed. J.S. Moore, 1979, p. 146. *See also:* <www.batharchivesco.uk>

City of Bath
Q.S. books, 1683-1785.
Court rolls, 1776-1971.
Court papers, 1786-1835.

Wells Town Hall.

City of Wells
Sessions books, 1600-21, 1625-50, 1671-1719, 1741-1757.
Calendars of prisoners tried at Wells and Taunton Q.S., 1870-79 (printed).
Convictions, 1856.

The King's Peace. The Justice's Notebooks of Thomas Horner, of Mells, 1770-1777, ed. Michael McGarrie (Soc. for LS, 1997).

STAFFORDSHIRE

Staffordshire Record Office, Stafford.

Catalogues of the various classes give brief descriptions of the documents with covering dates. There is a place name index to the order books, c.1690-1790, and a calendar to c.1635, both available only in the C.R.O.

See also
<Staffordshire.record.office@staffordshire.gov.uk>
and <Stoke.archives@stoke.gov.uk>

The only transcripts are those of edited Q.S. rolls, 1581-1609, in the *Staffordshire Historical Collections*, 6 vols., 1929-49.

County
Sessions bundles (i.e., documents produced in court at each session, too vaguely to specify contents):
Early series, 1668-1767;
Regular series from 1768.
Sessions minute books, 1687-1853.
Sessions order books, 1619-1877 (main series, gap 1667-1696).
Sessions rolls from 1581.
Calendars of prisoners, from 1768, in Sessions bundles; from 1840-1921, bound in volumes; indexed 1775-1820.
Process books, 1583-84, 1661-1743.
Recognizance rolls, 1668-1764 (not a complete series, but continued in Q.S. bundles).
Recognizance registers, 1687-1825.
Jury books, 1696-1702, 1789, 1851-73.
Alehouse keepers registers, 1782-1792.
Exemptions from office, 1786-1918.
Land Tax returns, 1781-1832 (see *LWTA*).
Electoral lists, 1832-1888 (see *ER*).
Sacrament certificates and subscriptions to oaths, 1673-1764 (with gaps).
Registration of Papists' estates 1715-40.
Register of deputations to gamekeepers, 1784-85; list of gamekeepers, 1790-91.

Stafford
Order books, 1744-83, 1825-36.

Lichfield Record Office.

See <lichfield.record.office@staffordshire.gov.uk>

City of Lichfield
Order books, 1726/7-1820, 1855-1971 [68, D25]; incl. jurors' lists.
Land Tax, 1819, 1825 [D25/3/2/5-6] (see *LWTA*).

Wolverhampton Archives & Local Studies.

See <www.wolverhampton.gov.uk/archives>

County Borough of Wolverhampton
Record books, 1864-1967.
Session books (drafts of above), 1864-1949.
Registers of orders for costs, 1864-1949.
Post trial prisoner calendars 1882-1965
Appeal book, 1864-1955.
Probation of Offenders' Act 1907: register of recogniz-ances, 1908-1949; register of probationers, 1908-12.
Indictments and recognizances, 1864-1971.
Coroners' inquests, 1864-1956 (but confidential for 75 years).

For poll books see *PB;* records of victuallers, see *VL*.

SUFFOLK

Suffolk Record Office, Ipswich.

Q.S. records for the County date from 1639, and there is a summary MS catalogue on cards. The only index is to the Order Book 1639-1651. Minute and Order Books 1639-1872 are on microfilm (11 reels) (available also at Bury St. Edmunds and Lowestoft branches) and can be purchased through E.P. Microforms Ltd.

See also <ipswich.ro@libher.suffolkcc.gov.uk>
or: <help@suffolklibraries.co.uk>

County
Minute and Order or Record books, incl. some draft volumes, 1639-1971.
Sessions rolls, 1682-1736.
Gaol registers: Beccles 1791-1848; Woodbridge 1802-42; Ipswich 1842-70.
Assize rolls, 1663-1695.
Land Tax for 1799 only (see *LWTA*).

Aldeburgh
Rolls, 1623-1635, 1712-1729. Minutes, 1689-1735.

Dunwich
Proceedings or minutes, 1696-1713, occasional years, 1720-1835.

Eye
Minutes, 1840-1862.
Informations, 1836-74, 1909, 1915-19.

Ipswich
Rolls, 1440-1544, 1722-1971 (also some 1572-1651, in Borough archives).
Books, 1509-15, 1549-1844.
Minutes, 1778-1809, 1841-1928.

Orford
Proceedings, 1704-1758.
Rolls, 1704-1733, 1753.

Suffolk Record Office, Bury St. Edmunds.

The only County Q.S. records, pre-1872, held are for highway diversions, from 1773.
See also <bury.ro@libher.suffolkcc.gov.uk.

Bury St. Edmunds
Books, 1694-1717, 1812-1958.
Files, 1673-1836 (gaps).
Depositions and informations, 1759-1817.
Oath rolls, 1714-1804, c.1848-1928.
Publicans' recognizances, 1799-1818 (see *VL*).

Sudbury
Books, 1579-1673, 1781-1836, 1851-1951.

Suffolk Record Office, Lowestoft.

See: <lowestoft.ro@libher.suffolkcc.gov.uk>

Southwold
Sessions books, 1800-1834.
Sessions papers, 1665-1747, 1833-1835.
Sacrament certificates, 1685-1763, 1785-1845.

For poll books and electoral registers, see *PB* and *ER;* for records of victuallers, see *VL*.

SURREY

Surrey History Centre, Woking.

See also: <shs@surreycc.gov.uk>

The Q.S. records were first described in *Q.S. Records with other records of the Peace for the County of Surrey*, comp. Miss J.L. Powell, ed. Hilary Jenkinson (Surrey C.C., 1931). All the records are now at the Surrey History Centre; however, some classes are known to have been destroyed (e.g. recognzance files from 1800, poll books 1790-1837) and others have not been identified.

The earliest Order Books and Sessions Rolls, 1659-1668, were published, *Q.S. Records*, 4 vols., ed. as above, 1934-8, Surrey C.C. and Surrey Record Society, and Surrey C.C. only, 1951 (1666-1668). These are of course indexed. These have been republished on fiche by the East Surrey FHS.

See also *Deposition Book of Richard Wyatt, J.P., 1767-1776*, ed. E. Silverthorne, Surrey R.S. **30**, 1978; this relates to north-west Surrey, the Chertsey and Egham area.

Transcripts and indexes to other records as shown.

County
Rolls, arranged by session, 1661-1800 (single sessions missing 1671, 1673, 1682, 1689, 1724, 1744, 1746, 1751). These include *inter alia* writs, jury lists, recognizances, indictments, presentments and sacrament certificates. Printed (with index) to 1668. Ts transcript 1669-1691, indexed. Ms transcript, Mids. 1694 - Easter 1695.

Surrey: *Surrey History Centre:* County *continued*

Recognizances 1801-88 have been destroyed, but recognizances, jury lists, oaths etc survive, 1889-1915.

Bundles, 1630, 1637, 1701-1888, less formal documents, mainly on paper and incl. gaol calendars and examinations and informations taken before Justices out of Court, filed separately. Detailed Ms list, 1701-1799, and index to list.

Order books, printed (with index), 1659-68, Ts transcript, 1669-1672, indexed in binders.

Minute books, from 1694-1971 (gap 1745-51).

Land Tax assessments, 1780-1831 (see *LWTA*).

Registers of electors, 1832-89 (*ER*).

Freeholders' lists 1696-1703, 1762-1824.

Licensing committee books: victuallers' recognizances; victuallers' registers 1785-1827 (see *VL*); slaughter houses.

Gamekeepers' deputations.

Borough of Guildford

Draft Court Book, 1698-1734.

Minute books, 1846-1971.

Sessions papers, 1745-1833.

Miscellaneous papers relating to administration of th pool law, 1750-1832.

Poor Law examinations, 1794-1836, with Ts calendar, indexed by C. Webb, West Surrey Family History Society.

Correspondence with the War office and Admiralty, incl. papers re. deserters, 1781-1817; billeting, 1785-1811; disputes between forces and civilian population, 1782-1812.

Magistrates' oaths, 1792-1820.

Papers connected with County Q.S. and Assizes, 1753-1823.

Royal Borough of Kingston upon Thames
(archives are made available, by appointment only, at the Local History Room, North Kingston Centre, Richmond Rd, Kingston KT2 5PE).

Sessions records are described in the *Guide to the Borough Archives* (1971, £1.40) . *See also:* <local.history@rbk.Kingston.gov.uk>

General files: 1668, 1685, 1688, 1690, 1692-94, 1708-48 (except 1710, 1720, 1732), incl. writ of summons, jury lists, presentments, some recognizances.

Second series, mainly presentments and recognizances, 1676-77, 1686, 1693, 1752-57, 1761, 1766-72.

City of London Records Office/L.M.A.

See p.21 and <ask.lma@corpoflondon.gov.uk>

Borough of Southwark

Files, 1667-1870.

Minute books, 1667-1768, 1785-1929.

Papers, 1654, 1667-1784, 1814-46 (incomplete).

The Records Office general subject card index gives particulars of certain classes of Sessions records. No other finding aids.

For poll books and electoral registers, see *PB* and *ER*; for records of victuallers, see *VL*.

SUSSEX

East Sussex Record Office, *Lewes.*

See also: <archives@eastsussex.gov.uk>
and <www.eastsussex.gov.uk/leisureand tourism/localandfamilyhistory>

Most of the Q.S. records for the whole county of Sussex (both East and West) are at the East Sussex R.O., as the two administrative counties of East and West Sussex were only formed in 1889, although for practical purposes the divisions had existed since at least the 16th century. The Q.S. records are admirably and in some detail described in *A Descriptive Report on the Q.S. ... Records in the custody of the County Councils of East and West Sussex,* by F.W. Steer.

Of finding aids, the Sussex Family History Group have published Settlement Orders and Cases (from Q.S. order books) for 1661-1749. There is also an alphabetically arranged Ms calendar of settlement papers and bastardy orders from Q.S. rolls, 1740-1770, at E.S.R.O.

E.S.R.O. has a slip index of *c.*11,000 East Sussex criminal cases before Q.S. Mainly from this, a list of East Sussex sentences of transportation at Q.S., 1740-1854 (827 names) has been published (Friends of E.S.R.O., £2.00 + p&p).

At **West Sussex Record Office**, there are card indexes to West Sussex defendants, 1791-1850, and transported convicts, 1778-1853.

The Order Book, 1642-1649, ed. B.C. Redwood, was published as Sussex Record Society, vol. **54**, 1954.

County
(asterisked items, relating to West Sussex, will also be found at *W.S.R.O.,* Chichester)

*Rolls, files and bundles, 1594-95, 1605-06, 1608-11, 1614-18, 1625-28, 1632-1950 (see *Report* for exact gaps for each division).

Indictment books, 1623-32, 1652-1789.

Fines and estreats, 1642-59, 1775-1859.

Order books, 1642-1833; Record books, 1833-1914 (facsimile of 1642-50 and microfilm of 1642-85, at *W.S.R.O.*).

Recognizance books, 1661-1836.

Minute books, 1673-1701, 1708-1805.

Process books etc., 1757-63, 1798-1903.

*Oaths of Allegiance and declarations, 1689-1866.

Register of dissenting ministers, 1689-1832 (card index).

Register of Quakers, 1716-53, 1855.

Sacrament certificates, 1702-1802.

Papists' oath rolls, 1778-1862.

*Register of Papists' estates, 1717-84.

*Land Tax assessments, 1780-1832 (see *LWTA*).

Register of gamekeepers' deputations, 1781-1928.

Victuallers' recognizances, 1781.

Corn dealers' declarations, 1821-38.

Rye
See *Records of Rye Corporation,* R.F. Dell, E.S.C.C., 1962, and in the Fifth *Report* of the Historical MSS. Comm., Part 1, p. 488 *et seq.*

Sussex *(E.S.R.O.) continued*

Winchelsea
See *Winchelsea Corporation Records*, R.F. Dell, E.S.C.C., 1963.
Court books, 1628-1734, 1769-1794.

Surviving records for other former boroughs in East Sussex (Pevensey, Seaford) are also at E.S.R.O. but are fragmentary.

Hastings
Rolls of oaths of JPs, 1819-67.
Persons tried, committed for trial and committed to gaol, 1824-33.
Orders re. transportation of convicts, 1823-27.
Grand jury presentments, 1662-91.
Gaol delivery, 1598-1679.
Hastings gaol books, 1838-54.
Coroners' inquests, 1665, 1667(2), 1771.
County rate books, 1796-1836.

West Sussex Record Office, *Chichester*
(see also County Q.S. records).

See: <records.office@westsussex.gov.uk>

Chichester
Rolls, 1577-1679, 1802-1834.
Minutes, 1754-1774, 1800-01, 1843-74.
Oath and sacrament certificates, 1723-1835.

For poll books and electoral registers, see *PB* and *ER*; for records of victuallers, see *VL*.

WARWICKSHIRE

Warwickshire County Record Office, *Warwick.*

Q.S. order books start in 1625, and the Q.S. proceedings for C17 (1625-1696) have been calendared and published in nine volumes in Warwick County Records series. Each volume has a very informative introduction and indexes of persons, places and subjects.

The Warwick County Records Series also contains one volume of Hearth Tax returns, 1662-74, for the Tamworth and Atherstone Divisions of Hemlingford Hundred (indexed). Personal names index (card and Ts) to remainder of 1674 return. Place names' index (persons under places) for southern part of county for whole period. Also the Warwick County Records Series vol. **1-5** covers the Quarter Sessions Order Book 1625-1674; vol. **6** Quarter Sessions Indictment Book 1631-1674; vol. **7-9** Quaret Sessions Proceedings 1674-1696.

Other Q.S. records have been briefly listed by class only.

See also: <recordoffice@warwickshire.gov.uk>

Tracing Your Ancestors in Warwickshire, June Watkins and Pauline Saul, B&MSGH, 1996, pp. 82-84 lists classes of Q.S. records (based on this Guide).

Warwickshire: *County Record Office, Warwick ctd.*

County
Order books 1625-1773; bundles 1774-C20.
Minutes, 1674-1877 (incl. gamekeepers' deputations, 1711-72).
Records of Q.S., 1878-C20.
Indictments, 1631-1760, 1834-43.
Recognizance books, 1731-40, 1757-59; lists 1797-1833.
Victuallers' recognizances, 1661, 1668-1707, 1735-40 (with gaps, some hundreds only), 1754-1829 (gaps) (see *VL*).
Gamekeepers' deputations, 1772-1898 (incl. alphabetical lists, 1789-1807).
Prisoners transported to North America 1772-76 [QS.118]. Calendar transcript in *Warwickshire History* (Warw. LH Soc) X.2 (Winter 1996/7) pp.71-81.
Popish recusants, lists 1680-84, 1690-94.
Papists' estates, 1717, 1719, 1723-24, 1731-45, 1747-64, 1768, 1778.
Freeholders and Jury Lists, 1696-C20.
Land Tax assessments, 1773-1832 (see *LWTA*).

Records relating specifically to **Coventry**, in main County series (see also *Coventry C.R.O.*, below):
Minutes, 1691-96, 1718-49, 1777-80, 1787-90, 1836-42;
Indictments, 1783-1842;
Recognizances, 1794-1842.

Warwick
Rolls (files), 1703-05, 1734-47, 1752-77, 1780-1836.
Q.S. book, 1768-1806.
Sacrament certificates, 1703-04, 1768-80.

Many of these records are of potential use to family historians. Not all are easy to use; there may be palaeographic difficulties or problems in connection with the way in which the documents have been preserved (some in bundles had a string passed through the centre of them, making them virtually unhandleable until they are separated, flattened and repaired).

Coventry Archives.

City of Coventry
Q.S. records date from 1449 (writs), and include:

Indictments, 1629-1813; files, 1770-1832;
Recognizance files, 1791-1832;
Sessions minute books, 1756-1825;
Nomination lists for surveyors, 1732-1833;
Jury lists, 1629-1750;
Constables' presentments, 1629-1739;
Settlement examinations and certificates 1716-48; removal orders, 1659-1812;
Transportation calendars etc., 1741-66;
Subscription roll for oaths of allegiance and supremacy, 1730-80;
Sacrament certificates, 1682-1828;
Land Tax assessments, 1740-1804 (see *LWTA*);
Licensed alehouse keepers, 1609 (see *VL*);
Licensing of victuallers, 1745-1835 (see *VL*);
Impressment of soldiers (1 vol.), 1744-5;
Offenders committed to the House of Correction, 1737;
Calendars of prisoners in gaol, 1819-47.

Warwickshire *continued*

See also: <archives@birmingham.gov.uk>

Birmingham

This Court was only established in 1839. Early records include:
Minute books, from 1839;
Registers of convictions, 1839-57.

The Shakespeare Birthplace Trust Record Office, Stratford upon Avon.

Stratford upon Avon

See *Descriptive Calendar of the Ancient Manuscripts and Records in the in possession of the Corporation of Stratford upon Avon*, Halliwell, 1863.

Proceedings, presentments, writs, summonses for jurors, jury lists etc., *c.*1602-74 (1 volume).
Further sessions books, 1672-1803, and unbound sessions files from 1729.
Sacrament certificates, 1732-50 (Halliwell, pp. 179-80), 1758-1806 and other oath rolls, 1734 on.
Victuallers' recognizances, 1763-1828 (see *VL*).

For poll books and electoral registers, see *PB* and *ER*; for records of victuallers, see *VL*.

WESTMORLAND

Cumbria Record Office, Kendal.

See also: <www.cumbria.gov.uk/archives>

The County Q.S. rolls, are calendared up to 1813, with subject index and list of selected documents, e.g. removal orders, bastardy papers etc. There are lists of other Q.S. records.
A unique 'census' of 1787, compiled by order of the Q.S., has been published as *Vital Statistics: The Westmorland 'Census' of 1787*, ed. L. Ashcroft, Cumbria Record Office (Kendal), 1992. Full details are given in *Local Census Listings, 1522-1930*, Gibson and Medlycott, 3rd ed., F.F.H.S., 1997/2001.

County

Order books, 1669-1971 (gap 1799-1810).
Indictment books, 1656-1971 (gap 1788-1810).
Rough minute and memoranda books, 1733-1916.
Sessions rolls (arranged by year and by session within each year), 1726, 1729-1971.
Jurors' books, 1775 on.
Poll books, 1820, 1826, 1832 (see *PB*).
Land Tax assessments, 1765, 1773, 1790, 1793, 1809, 1823, 1826, 1831, 1832 (not for all wards) (see *LWTA*).
Electoral registers, 1832-1973 (see *ER*).
Transportation bonds, 1739-1785.
List of inhabitants, 1787 (most north Westmorland) (published, see above).
Kendal corn rent maps with schedules, 1836.

Kendal

Order and indictment books, 1685-1731, 1815-1835.

WILTSHIRE

Wiltshire and Swindon History Centre, Chippenham

N.B. The new History Centre is located in Cocklebury Road, Chippenham, opened in October 2007.

See also <WSRO@wiltshire.gov.uk>
and <history.wiltshire.gov.uk/heritage/index.htm>

The Q.S. records are described in the *Guide to the Records in the Custody of the Clerk of the Peace for Wiltshire*, M.G. Rathbone, Wilts. C.C., 1959 (80p); also in *Records of Q.S. in the County of Wilts.* (Report on MSS. in various collections, **1** , pp. 65-176), Historical MSS. Commission, 1901.
There are published abstracts in:
Minutes of Proceedings in Sessions, 1563 and 1574 to 1592, H.C. Johnson, Wilts. Record Society, **4**, 1949.
Records of the County of Wilts., being Extracts from the Q.S. Great Rolls of the 17th century, 1603-1699, 2 vols., B.H. Cunnington, 1929-32.
Wiltshire Q.S. and Assizes, 1736, J.P.M. Fowle, Wilts. R.S. **11**,1955.
'Extracts from the Records of the Wiltshire Q.S.', R.W. Merriman, *Wilts. Arch. Magazine*, **20-22**.
The Wiltshire FHS has published the following *"Goodness and Badness" an index of the calendars of prisoner, Wiltshire Quarter Sessions*. Vol **1** 1722-1820 vol **2** 1820-1830. *A miscellany of bastardy records for Wiltshire*, vol 1 1728-1893. *Rough justice, summary convictions in Wiltshire*. In 12 vols. Covering the period 1698-1903.

County

Great Rolls, 1603-1955 (complete except for occasional years in C17). They include jury lists, presentments, indictments, recognizances, writs, depositions (to 1828, then a separate class), petitions, sacrament certificates (1673-1827).
Insolvent debtors, 1724-81 (with gaps).
Calendars of prisoners, 1728-46, 1757-82, 1812-17, 1828-38, 1841-82 (see also Great Rolls).
Removal orders, 1737-1775.
Depositions, 1828-1905 (see also Great Rolls).
Entry Books: Minutes, 1563, 1574-92, 1598-1604, 1610-77, 1688-1823, 1864-1951; rough minutes, 1745-1897.
Order Books, 1642-1755.
Process books of indictments and presentment, 1661-1857 (with gaps).
Oaths: against Transubstantiation, 1689-90; rolls, 1704-41 (Test Act); of Allegiance etc., 1730-1864.
Dissenting ministers or teachers, 1689-1811, 1822, 1827-29.
Papists, 1778, 1791-1812, 1829-30.
Dissenters' places of worship: certificates, 1695-1745, 1795, 1814-50.
Jurors, 'Freehold Books', 1708, 1713, c.1725, 1731-1732, 1734-42, 1744-48, 1761-62, 1774-6, 1783-1857 etc.; returns, 1699, 1781, 1836 (some Hundreds only).
Gamekeepers' deputations, 1711-1939; alphabetical list, 1731-1941.

Wiltshire (Wilts & Swindon R.O.): *County contd*

Papists' estates, rolls/registers, 1717-1788.
Transportation of felons, bonds and contracts, 1717-20, 1778-79.
Licensed victuallers: recognizances, 1737-59 (gaps); registers 1753, 1756-61, 1822-27; original recognizances 1808, 1841, 1828 (see *VL*).
Elections: Poll books, 1772, 1790, 1818, 1819, 1833, 1837 (see *PB*).
'Marriage' Tax, 1697-1705 (see *HT*).
Land Tax assessments, 1773-74, 1780-1833 (see *LWTA*).
Prisons: prisoners at Devizes, 1822.

Devizes
Minute books, 1657-1663.
Register of convictions, 1842-on.

Marlborough [WRO G/22]
Clerks' notebook, 1585-1624.
Minute books, 1711-20, 1772-1835.
Examinations, informations, presentments etc., 1707-1846.

Salisbury
Q.S. rolls, 1761-1971.
Minute books, 1747-1971.
Other miscellaneous records from C18.

For electoral registers, see *ER*; for records of victuallers, see *VL*.

WORCESTERSHIRE

Worcestershire Record Office, Worcester.

See also: <RecordOffice@worcestershire.gov.uk>

Full calendar of Q.S. rolls, 1591-1643, by J. Willis-Bund, pubd. Worcs. Hist. Soc., 1900, fully indexed. Finding aids include Q.S. Rolls, 1651-1849 (including place, personal name and subject index); index to Highways references contained in the County of Worcestershire Q.S. Order Books, 1821-1959; Index to Gamekeepers Deputations (listed by Lord, Manor and Gamekeeper, 1734-1807); Index to Sessions Orders, 1852-1880 (Ref b118, BA 771).

County
Rolls from 1590, published to 1646, largely continuous, but gap in Sessions' packets, 1646-1651.
Order Books continuous from 1693, indexed 1693-1833.
Indictments, recognizances, calendars of prisoners, minute books, licensing papers.
Calendars of prisoners (indexed 1839-56).
Land Tax from 1781 (placename index, 1780-1832) Also post 1832 (1797-1949, with gaps) (see *LWTA*).

Worcestershire: *Worcs. R.O., County contd.*

There are many lists within these records, such as jury lists, prisoner lists, lists of electors (see *ER*); however, most are not indexed in any way, and juries and prisoners for the earlier period (1590-1800) are difficult to isolate.

City of Worcester
Sessions papers, 1710-on.
Sessions books.
Recorder's notebook; Treasurer's accounts; Calendars of prisoners; Minutes; Jurors' books; Clerk of the Peace notebooks.

For poll books, see *PB*; for records of victuallers, see *VL*.

YORK

York City Archives.

See also: <archives@york.gov.uk>

City of York
Q.S. records are described in a handlist of York City records, *A Catalogue of the Charters, House Books, etc.*, William Giles, 1909, on which the following list is based.

Minutes, 1559-99, 1616-19, 1638-75, 1686-1869, 1900-71.
Draft minutes, 1659-92, 1711-19.
Plaint books, 1718-1783.
Court books, 1716-1753.
Court papers, 1721-23, 1727-39, 1742-43, 1746-74.
Declarations, pleadings etc., 1711-17, 1720-44.
Judgement papers, 1715-17, 1721-32, 1734-44.
Recognizances (mainly alehouse), 1531-41, 1550-52, 1646-48, 1656, 1660, 1662-63, 1674, 1688, 1720-37, 1745-57, 1763, 1765-80, 1782,90, 1792-96, 1801-03, 1807(see *VL*).
Persons tried at Q.S. with sentences, 1819-1833.
Calendars of prisoners, 1828-1853.
Convictions by Justices out of sessions, 1824-1853.
York Assize Calendars 1824-1838 (gaps)

North Yorkshire Record Office, Northallerton.

Calendar of prisoners, York City Q.S., 1861-64.

For Hearth Tax, other late C17 taxes, Land Tax assessments, poll books and electoral registers, see *HT, LWTA, PB* and *ER*; for records of victuallers, see *VL*.

YORKSHIRE: EAST RIDING

> ### East Riding of Yorkshire Archives Office, Beverley.

See also: <archives.services@eastriding.gov.uk>

East Riding

Sessions files, 1706-C20 (Ts index, 1766-1799);
Indictments, recognizances, examinations, petitions and convictions kept separately after 1800.
Order books, 1647-1651, 1708-C20.
Recognizance books, 1786-1903.
Enrolment books, to include papists' estates in earlier years, 1717-1883.
Freeholders and jury lists, 1757, 1781, 1789, 1808-1921 (gaps).
Oath rolls, 1714-1971.
Insolvent debtors' papers, 1729-1829.
Bastardy recognizances and orders, 1800-1840.
Game preservations, 1768-1911.
Licensed tradesmen, 1745-1876.
Land Tax assessments, 1782-1832 (see *LWTA*).
Indexes to prisoners tried and convicted, 1735-1971 (contemporary);
Lists of admissions, discharges and deaths in private asylums, 1828-1864 (Ts).

Earlier police records are included under Q.S. references. Useful genealogical sources are the appointment books etc. of the East Riding (1857-1968) and Beverley (1843-1927) Constabularies (restriction on access to more recent volumes). Printed index to cover Beverley volumes and East Riding up to 1919.

Hedon

Minute books, 1657-1860.
Sacrament certificates, 1742-1825.
Alehouse recognizances, 1758-1828 (see *VL*).

Beverley

Sessions files and draft minutes, 1719, 1728-1796.
Briefs and proceedings, 1717, 1819-1841.
Minutes, 1785-1836.
Indictments, 1719-1836.
Sacrament certificates, 1719-1805.
Oath rolls, 1754-1907 (some gaps).

> ### Hull City Archives
> (separate handlists available).

See also: <city.archives@hullcc.gov.uk>

Kingston upon Hull

Until 1835 the couny of Kingston upon Hull, informally known as Hullshire, included the parishes of Hessle, Kirkella and North Ferriby. After 1835 these became part of the East Riding of Yorkshire.

Sessions order books from 1693 (gap 1846-57).
Minute books, 1842-1971.
Recorders' note books, 1875-1971.
Rolls/bundles, from 1741, include:
Insolvent debtors' papers;

Yorkshire: East Riding: *Hull City Archives* contd.

Contracts for transportation of felons, 1757-75 (published by East Yorks. F.H.S.);Affiliation papers, 1806-29;
Vagrancy and pauper removals, 1741-1841.
Indictments from 1741 and witness statement, from 1840 in respect of criminal cases to 1899;
Coroners' inquests verdicts and witness statements 1840-99;
Colonial service agreements, 1749-57;
Printers' notices, 1807-46;
Lists of freemasons, 1799-1843;
Returns of pauper lunatics from 1829.
Taxation assessments, C16-1827 (many gaps), including Marriage Tax, 1695-97 (published) (see *HT, LWTA*).

For poll books and electoral registers, see *PB* and *ER*; for records of victuallers, see *VL*.

YORKSHIRE: NORTH RIDING

> ### North Yorkshire County Record Office, Northallerton.

See also <www.northyorks.gov.uk>
or: <archives.northyorks.gov.uk>

There is a printed calendar of Q.S. minute books in *Q.S. records: North Riding*, by J.C. Atkinson, North Riding Record Society, **1-9** (1884-92), contents:
1. **1605-12**, abstracts or transcripts of all minutes and orders, incl. special sessions. Continued in following volumes, except that details of petty larcenies, common assualts, trifling robberies, and other minor offences, are omitted.
2. **1612-20**, incl. special sessions, with extracts from accounts for lame soldiers and hospitals, 1605-1615.
3. **1621-34**, incl. special sessions; recusants, 1611-1630.
4. **1634-47**, incl. enrolled indentures, 1538-1693.
5. **1647-58.**
6. **1658-77.**
7. **1677-1716**, with registrations of papists' lands, 1717-42.
8. Registration of papists' lands, 1717-82; oaths of allegiance and supremacy, 1766-77; declarations of dissenting preachers, 1791-1818.
9. More papists lists, incl. enrolments of conveyances, 1719-1770 ; persons taking oaths, 1698-1716.

The C.R.O. has Ts lists of other and later records, and an index of bundles. Descriptive lists published in North Yorks. R.O. Annual Reports, 1968 (administrative records), 1969 (enrolled records) and 1970 (court and financial records).
Q.S. records available for consultation in the form of microfilm or calendars are listed in *Guide No. 1*. These include minute and order books, 1570, 1605-1881, and sessions bundles, 1660-1888 (incomplete).

Yorkshire: North Riding:
North Yorkshire County Record Office ctd.

North Riding
Minute and order books from 1605 (complete; also one roll, 1570); published calendar, see above, but note that this is less comprehensive in its later volumes.

Separate minutes (trials and judicial business) from 1769.

Sessions bundles, 1660-C20.

Calendars of prisoners: York Castle, 1765-94, 1827-1834, 1843; Scarborough, 1852, 1890-1902; York assizes, 1832-45; York city Q.S., 1861-64; Northallerton, 1790-1803, 1813, 1817-99; drafts, 1811-67.

Yorkshire assizes calendars, 1855-1937.

Transportation, draft orders, C18-1866; to America, 1736-74.

Insolvent debtors' papers, 1724-1833.

Poll books: county, 1807, 1830; North Riding, 1835 (see *PB*).

Registers of electors, 1832-1974. (see also *ER*).

Land Tax assessments: Birdforth, 1692-1765; all wapentakes, 1781-1832 (some gaps) (see *LWTA*).

Registers of deputations to gamekeepers, 1797-1960; certificates for killing game (incl. gamekeepers and lords of manors), 1784-99.

Register of hairpowder certificates, 1795-97.

Jurors/freeholders' books: *c.*1729, 1743, 1750-1847 (gaps).

Licensed tradesmen: victuallers and alehouse keepers, 1717-20, 1758, 1774-1808, 1811, 1822-1829.

Nonconformist chapels, 1829, 1836.

Dissenting ministers' declarations, C17-1818.

Papists' estates, 1717-1781 (see published volumes, above).

Sacrament certificates, 1755-1810.

Other oaths, 1689-1838.

Register of constables, c.1859.

Richmond
Sessions files, 1627-28, 1700-1722, 1774-1837.

Indictments, 1770-1835.

Sacrament certificates, 1695-1717.

Oaths, 1696-1870.

Alehouse keepers' recognizances, 1715-1828.

Scarborough
Minute books, 1696-1723, 1778-1869, 1875-78.

West Yorkshire Archive Service: Wakefield.

Liberty of Ripon
Justices of peace, 1737-1950.

Court in session, 1632-1920.

Clerk of the peace, 1740-1901.

Enrolment, registration and deposit, 1770-1896.

'Court military', 1716-1846.

YORKSHIRE: WEST RIDING

West Yorkshire Archive Service: Wakefield.

See also: ,archives@wyjs.org.uk> *or* <wakefield@wyjs.org.uk>

See *Guide to the Quarter Sessions records of the West Riding of Yorkshire, 1637-1971, and other official records,* by B.J. Barber, W.Y. Archive Service, 1984. Each Order Book and Indictment Book is indexed.

Other publications: *West Riding Sessions Rolls, 1597-1602,* Yorks. Arch. Soc., Record Series **3**, 1888.

West Riding Sessions Records, Part 2, Orders, 1611-1642, Indictments, 1637-1642, Yorks. Arch. Soc. Record Series, **54**, 1914. These volumes contain transcriptions of records no longer extant.

West Riding
Order books, 1638-1647, 1647-49, 1653-1971.

*Indictment books, 1637-1642, 1647-1971.

Q.S.files, 1662, 1665-1971.

*Land Tax duplicates, 1781-1832 (see *LWTA*).

*Electoral registers, 1840-1889 (continued in West Riding County Council series to 1974) (see *ER*).

*Register of Roman Catholic Estates, 1717-1789.

Asterisked records are of direct use to genealogists. The Land Tax returns are arranged by township.

The West Yorkshire Archive Service H.Q. also holds records for the **Liberty of Ripon** (see 'North Riding') and for the **Liberty of Cawood, Wistow and Otley,** 1720-1864.

West Yorkshire Archive Service: Leeds, Sheepscar, Leeds.

See also <leeds@wyjs.org.uk>

Leeds
The only pre-C19 Q.S. records to survive are Order and Indictment Books, 1698-1809, 1844-1967, some with subject and name indexes in the books. All rolls and papers are apparently lost.

Doncaster Archives Department.

See A *Guide to Doncaster Archives.,* 2001;.*see also:* <doncaster.archives@doncaster.gov.uk>

Borough of Doncaster
Proceedings, 1520-1600, 1685-1688, 1725-1730, 1795-1825, 1842-1971.

Indictments, recognizances, jury lists and other sessions papers, C17-C18.

Sessions rolls, 1919-1971.

For poll books, see *PB*; for records of victuallers, see *VL*.

ANGLESEY

Anglesey County Record Office, Llangefni.

See also: <www.ynysmon.gov.uk> [in Welsh only]

County

The Q.S. records for Anglesey date from 1772. There are no finding aids for the majority of the collection, although work on these is in progress. The judicial papers for the years 1772-1824 and 1830-1889 have now been catalogued, some indexed. (subject, place and surname) completed or in preparation. The intervening 1823-1849 was due to be completed by 1994. Some administrative papers, including those of Beaumaris gaol, have also been catalogued and indexed. Copies of such lists are also available at the Caernarfon and Dolgellau area offices.

Of the Q.S. rolls, some remain in their original form, but others had been broken up prior to being received into custody, administrative papers separated from judicial, with judicial papers being filed according to quarter.

Records of interest to family historians include:

Electoral lists, 1832-1889, 1897, 1919 onwards (see *ER*);
Poll books, 1784-1837 (see *PB*).
Parliamentary election poll books, 1784, 1837;
Order books, 1768-1971;
Recognizance books, 1795-1832;
Beaumaris gaol records, 1820-1879 (indexed);
Land Tax assessments, 1712-1869 (see *LWTA*);
Window Tax, 1751-1786 (see *LWTA*).
Poor, 1788-1816.
Jury lists, 1840-1901

An article on 'The Anglesey Q.S. Records', by Hugh Owen, was published in the *Anglesey Antiquarian Society Transactions*, 1925, pp. 69-114.

Q.S. records for the **Borough of Beaumaris** are in the archives of the **University College of North Wales, Bangor**, ranging in date from 1650 to 1836. Finding aids are available, ref. nos. 'Beaumaris and Anglesey Records II, 24-49'.

BRECONSHIRE or BRECKNOCKSHIRE

Powys County Archives Office, Llandrindod Wells.

(records transferred in 1990 from the National Library of Wales)

See also: <archives@powys.gov.uk>

Sessions rolls, 1690-1968.
Recognizance rolls, 1820-47, 1871.
Order books, 1670-1956.
Lists of constables, 1844-1849.
Police pay returns/sheets, 1859-1883, 1895-96.
Register of electors for County, 1836-92, Brecon, 1852 (see also *ER*); Lists of voters, 1839-1859.

Breconshire *continued*

Poll book, 1837 (see also *PB*).
Jurors' books, 1825-26, 1865.
Returns of jurors, 1728, 1810, 1825, 1843-1853, 1910-11, 1914.
Oath books, 1714-1909.
Sacrament certificates, 1691-1707.
Calendars of prisoners, 1836-1912.

CAERNARVONSHIRE

Caernarfon Record Office, (Gwynedd Archives and Museums Service), Caernarfon.

See also: <archives.caernarfon@gwynedd.gov.uk>

The Q.S.records for the County are described in the *Guide to the Caernarvonshire Record Office*, 1952.

The earliest records are printed in a Calendar, 1541-1558, ed. W. Ogwen Williams (Caernarvonshire Hist. Soc. for C. Joint Records C'tee of Q.S. and C.C., 1956), which has a long introduction (also published separately under the title *Tudor Gwynedd*).

At the C.R.O. there is a card index to the Calendar and catalogues.

County

Indictment rolls, 1541-42.
Sessions rolls, 1546-88, 1608-60, 1666, 1668-71, 1673-74, 1676, 1680-81, 1685-86, 1698-C20 (incl. list, licences and recognizances for alehouse and alehouse keepers; calendars of prisoners; constables; debtors; depositions: informations and examinations; drovers' licences; indictments; returns of freeholders qualified to serve on juries; jury panels and lists; petitions; recognizances; sacrament certificates; settlement papers, mainly from mid-C18, incl. many warrants for removal of Irish paupers, 1740-50).
Recognizance rolls and books, 1543-69 (gaps), 1575, 1612-13, 1633, 1649-50, 1672-73, 1803-65.
Order books, 1684-90, 1716-18, 1721, 1752-54, 1756-88, 1815-1922, 1932-37.
Indictment and presentment book, 1723-34.
Alehouse recognizance book, 1626-28 (see *VL*).
Dissenters' meeting houses, registration, 1794 (see also Order Books).
Gamekeepers' certificates, 1784-90; deputations, 1786-1888.
Hearth Tax, 1662 (see *HT*).
Jurors: Freeholders' books, 1733-49.
Land Tax assessments, 1746-1830 (see *LWTA*).
Registers of oaths, 1704-1858.
Sacrament registers, 1727-1831.

For poll books and electoral registers, see *PB* and *ER*; for records of victuallers, see *VL*.

CARDIGANSHIRE

Cardinganshire/Ceredigion Record Office,
Aberystwyth.

See also: <archives@ceredigion.gov.uk>

The only early Q.S. records for the County are Order Books, dating from 1739.

For Land Tax assessments, poll books and electoral registers, see *LWTA*, *PB* and *ER*.

CARMARTHENSHIRE

Carmarthenshire Archives Service, *Carmarthen.*

The few **County** Q.S.records to survive are listed briefly in *Carmarthenshire Record Office: Survey of archive holdings*, 1980. The only early records are the Order or Minute Books, 1748-1752, 1794-1813, 1820-1971.

Carmarthen Borough Q.S. records are also at the C.R.O. listed in the *Survey*, but nothing significant pre-C19.

For Land Tax assessments, poll books and electoral registers, see *LWTA*, *PB* and *ER*.

See also: <Archives@carmarthenshire.gov.uk>

DENBIGHSHIRE

National Library of Wales, *Aberystwyth*

Denbighshire Q,S. Records (Chirk Castle estate):
Rolls, 1643-1699;
Test Act registers and certificastes 1673-1690;
Assessments and taxes, 1628-1811;
Highways and bridges, 1665-1795;
Maimed soldiers, 1662-1680.

Another Order Book, 1675-88, is in the **British Library** [Add. MS 40175] (photocopies at Ruthin and N.L.W.).

Denbighshire Record Office, *Ruthin.*

See also: <archives@denbighshire.gov.uk>

The Record Office holds Q.S. records for **Denbighshire** and for the borough of **Denbigh** and both collections have been fully listed. The **County** Q.S. records are described in *Handlist of Denbighshire Q.S. Records* (2 vols.), 1991.

County (very extensive)
Minute and order books, 1714-1959.
Sessions rolls, 1706-1971.
Qualification records, 1745-1930.
Recognizance book, 1649-95.
Insolvent debtors, 1772-1833.
Prosecution books, 1844-92.
Depositions, 1866-89 (and earlier in sessions rolls).
Transportation bonds, 1733-1774.
Sacrament certificates, 1706-1826.
Oaths of Allegiance, 1711-1868.
Register of papists' estates, 1716-1759.
Land Tax assessments, 1778-1831 (see *LWTA*).

Denbighshire *continued*

Freeholders' books and lists, 1756-1824.
Jurors' books and lists, 1825-1910.
Registers of electors, 1832-1971 (not a complete series) (see *ER*).
Gamekeepers' deputations, 1767-1926.
Alehouse recognizances, 1733-1828 (see *VL*).
General and special accounts, 1698-1914: incl. treasurers' accounts, 1698-1885; bills and vouchers, 1747-1889; police accounts, 1840-1889; militia accounts, 1761-1817; prosecution allowances, 1784-1914.
Bridge bonds, 1696-1884 (indexed).
Deposited plans, 1792-1965.

Denbigh
These are described in the *Handlist of the Denbigh Borough Records* (Clwyd Record Office Handlist **1**, 1975).

Minute books, 1769-1835.
Recognizance books, 1812-1835.
Sessions papers, incl. jury lists, presentments, depositions etc., 1790-1835.

For poll books, see *PB*; for records of victuallers, see *VL*.

FLINTSHIRE

Flintshire Record Office, *Hawarden.*

See <www.flintshire.gov.uk> *and for online collections list:* <www.archivesnetworkwales.info>

The Q.S. records for the County date only from 1720, and, such as they are, are described in the admirable *Guide to the Flintshire Record Office*, by A.G. Veysey, Flints. C.C., 1974. The earlier *Handlist of County Records* (1955) is still of value for its account of justices of the peace and for transcripts of selected records.
The Record Office published a calendar of Sessions Rolls, 1747-1752, ed. by Derrick Pratt, in 1983 (£3.75 + p&p).

County
Minute books, 1720-1893, 1901-1962.
Sessions rolls from 1747 (some gaps).

Few other records, no Land Tax assessments, jury or electors lists etc.

For poll books and electoral regiisters, see *PB* and *ER*.

GLAMORGAN

Glamorgan Record Office, *Cardiff.*

See also: <GlamRO@cardiff.ac.uk>

County
Minute or order books, 1719-1972.
Rolls, 1727-1971.
Register of alehouse recognizances, 1753-63 (see *VL*).
Register of badgers 1756-64.

Glamorgan *continued*

Recognizance books and rolls, 1779-1970.
Process book, 1739-1821
Indictments and presentments, 1730-1846.
Calendars of prisoners, 1850-1971.
Jurors lists 1826-36, 1847-50, some years between 1873 and 1921.
Commissions of the Peace, 1761-1974.
Qualification books, 1757-1970.
Order books, 1729-1791.
Gamekeepers' deputations, 1785-1831 (gaps).
Land Tax assessments, 1781-1831, and some earlier from 1766 (see *LWTA*).
Registers of electors, 1843 on (see *ER*).

Very few pre-C20 records survive for Cardiff Borough Q.S.

For poll books, see *PB*.

MERIONETH

> **Merioneth Archives/Archifdy Meironnydd**
> **Archives** *(Gwynedd Archives and Museums Service), Dolgellau.*

See also: <archives.dolgellau@gwynedd.gov.uk>

There is a published *Calendar of the Merioneth Q.S. Rolls, 1733, 1743-65* (gaps), ed. by Keith Williams-Jones (out of print).
Records from 1776-1792, 1800-53, 1860-79, are also calendared or catalogued.

County
Sessions Rolls for 1733, 1743-89 (some individual sessions missing, but no years completely missing except 1785), 1790-on, calendared or catalogued.
Order books from 1787.

Records include rolls, files, writs, jury lists, but no pre-1832 Land Tax assessments.

For electoral registers, see *ER*.

MONMOUTHSHIRE

> **Gwent Record Office, Cwmbran.**

See also: <gwent.records@torfaen.gov.uk>

The *Guide to the Monmouthshire Record Office*, by W.H. Baker (1959, now o.p.), lists all classes of Q.S. records. A list of Q.S. records is now available as a separate *Guides to Research*. There are detailed lists or indexes available in the R.O. to classes below that are asterisked:

County
*Minute books, 1769-89, 1799-1855, 1870-1929.
Record books, in general duplicating Minute books, but covering the missing 1855-1870 period.
*Process books, 1719-1844.
Jury panels, 1809-1854.
Recognizances, 1790-1936.

Monmouthshire *continued*

Indictments and presentments, 1780-1949.
*Grand Jury presentments, 1802-29.
Depositions, 1818-1842.
Calendars of prisoners, 1808-1936.
Insolvent debtors' papers, 1796-1847.
*Land Tax assessments, 1793-1832 (see *LWTA*).
*Alehouse recognizances, 1810-1825 (see *VL*).
*Oaths and declarations, various, from 1763.

Monmouth Borough
Draft minutes of proceedings, 1822-1836.
Depositions, 1778-1836.
Recognizances, 177-1835.
Records of conviction, 1825-1830.
Book of complaints and informations, 1829-1830.
Presentments of petty constables and juries, 1770-1835.

Newport Borough
Process book, 1733-1783.
Minute book, 1760-1813.

For poll books and electoral registers, see *PB* and *ER*; for records of victuallers, see *VL*.

MONTGOMERYSHIRE

> **Powys County Archives Office, Llandrindod Wells.**

(records transferred in 1990 from the National Library of Wales).
See also: <archives@powys.gov.uk>

County
Rolls, 1719-1971 (some gaps, but almost complete from mid-C18).
Order books, 1707-1737, 1759-84, 1797-1813, 1822-1833 (incomplete), 1833-1913; draft order book, 1814-1818.
Memorial roll for registration as voters by right of annuity or rent charge, 1774-1810.
Land Tax assessments for Montgomery Upper Division, 1792, and Machynlleth hundred, 1794 (see *LWTA*).
Electoral registers: County, 1887; Boroughs, 1861-1876.
Oaths of allegiance, 1755-1869 (incomplete).
Freeholders' book, jurors, 1776.
Returns for jury service, 1769.
Justices' qualification rolls, 1831-1901.
Returns of justices, 1801.
Return of prisoners for trial, 1834-1849.
Return of lunatic paupers for Dolgellau Union (co. Mont.), 1866.
Parish assessment lists (incomplete), 1895.

> **National Library of Wales, Aberystwyth.**

An account of some C17 Q.S. records amongst the Wynnstay estate collection is given in 'A Schedule of Q.S. Records of the County of Montgomery at the N.L.W.', by Professor E.A. Lewis, *Collections Historical and Archaeological relating to Montgomeryshire*, **46** (1940), 156-82; **47** (1941), 26-60.

Montgomeryshire (N.L.W.) *continuee*

Part 1 gives a detailed but not necessarily complete list and abstract of records for single sessions surviving for 1614, 1620, 1629, 1633, 1635, 1636 and 1640. Contents include returns of bailiffs, names of jurors and officers, warrants, recognizances of the Peace, ale recognizances and presentments of licensed victuallers.

Part 2 briefly lists records, for **Machynlleth Hundred** only, for 1659-62, 1706-07, 1711-24, 1732-35.

[Welsh]Pool borough

Powis Castle collection:
Estreats, 1672-74; 1676, 1691-92 (with Montgomery);
Files and papers, 1706-2.

Llanfyllin borough

See 'Miscellaneous documents [in the Powis Castle collection] concerning the borough of Llanfyllin', by Professor E.A. Lewis, Mont. Coll. (1937), 61-100. These include:
Oath rolls, 1674-1754 (10) (published);
Files and papers, 1695-1762, 1820;
Sacrament certificates, 1707-61 (published).

For poll books, see *PB*.

PEMBROKESHIRE

Pembrokeshire Record Office, *Haverfordwest.*
(tel. 01437 763707)

Finding aids consist of lists. Some of the Pembroke-shire Sessions Rolls have been calendared, 1779-1785. There is a nominal index to prisoners at the county gaol, 1813-1832.

Contact: <Claire.Orr@Pembrokeshire.gov.uk>

County of Pembrokeshire

Order books, 1734-1834.
Sessions rolls, 1779-1971.
Minute books, 1783-1971.
Indictment book, 1818-1865.
Royal pardons and remissions, 1825-1863.
Estreats of fines, 1805-1834.
Lists of those eligible to serve as jurors, 1790-1921.
Poll books, 1812-1831 (see *PB*).
Electoral lists and registers, 1832-1887 (see *ER*).
Land Tax assessments, 1786-1831 (see *LWTA*).
Commissions of the Peace, 1773-1973.
Lists of Justices, 1808-1989 [with gaps].
Qualification oaths and declarations, 1761-1973.
Deposited plans, 1844-1970.
Enclosure awards, 1786-1863.
Calendars of prisoners at Great Sessions and Assizes, Registers of prisoners at the county gaol, 1813-1863.
Prisoners' committal and discharge papers, 1812-1864.
Lists of lunatics, 1828-1925.

Pembrokeshire *continued*

Lists of alehouse keepers, 1810-1813.
Register of alehouses and alehouse recognizances, 1822-1828.
Register of boats on inland waterways, 1795.
Records of insolvent debtors, 1795-1874.
Freeholders books, 1789-1837.
Freemasons returns, 1873-1894.
Appointments of gamekeepers, 1784-1831.
County of the town of Haverfordwest
Sessions rolls, 1782-1951.
Minutes, 1843-1951.
Land Tax assessments, 1802-1823 [with gaps] (see *LWTA).*
Jury lists, 1895-1916.
Register of electors, 1840 and 1880.
Qualification oaths and declarations, 1786-1949.

For records of victuallers, see *VL.*

RADNORSHIRE

Powys County Archives Office, *Llandrindod Wells.*

(records transferred in 1990 from the National Library of Wales).
See <archives@powys.gov.uk>

County

Rolls, 1753-1951.
Order books, 1771-1951.
List of debtors, 1797.
Returns of prisoners for trial, 1815-1829.
Calendars of prisoners, 1831, 1836, 1898.
Lists of constables for Colwyn hundred, 1854, 1871.
Oaths of allegiance by JPs and others, 1779-1812, 1903-1911.
Land Tax assessments, 1812-17, 1821-31 (see *LWTA).*
Lists of freeholders, 1775, 1815-1817.
Lists of persons for jury service, 1794, 1817-1824 (incomplete), 1876-1912.
Returns of persons liable to serve as chief constables, 1815-1825, 1832-1838 (incomplete).
Jurors books, 1902-1949.
Returns of lunatics (various parishes), 1833, 1836; and of unsound mind, 1889-1893.
Lists of pauper lunatics at joint counties asylum Abergavenny, 1880-1890.
Poll clerk's books, 1841.
Registers of electors, 1868-1915 (incomplete), 1918-1926 (see *ER*).
List of innkeepers, 1815.
Register of gamekeepers, 1845-1870.

See also 'Records of Radnorshire General Sessions at the Shire Hall, Presteigne', by W.H. Howse, *The Radnorshire Society Transactions,* **13-14**.

For poll books, see *PB*.